FANCY BEING PAID FOR THIS

Billie Smith

I am grateful to Maggie Shearer the illustrator, and to Elizabeth Candlish, Margaret Hubbard, and Pete Buwert who gave me practical help and encouragement.

ISBN 978-1-4461-0021-9

READ THIS FIRST

In the 1970's Edinburgh's Education Department was innovative and forward looking, one of the first Scottish authorities to be aware that the education of high school students could be far more effective if they had the help they needed to help them deal with the social and domestic problems many of them faced. Poverty, family breakups, chronic illness or addiction in the home, and parental unemployment were some of the issues that inhibited youngsters from benefiting from their schooling. The appointment of guidance teachers would provide every pupil in school with a mentor who, aware of the issues each one faced, could offer the support and counselling needed.

One of Edinburgh's first guidance teachers, I was lucky to work for almost all of my twenty-four years in a high school under an innovative, child-centred head who in filling guidance posts attempted to choose teachers with an aptitude for and genuine interest in the pupils' welfare, and he thoroughly supported them. We found working in an area of multiple deprivation demanding and challenging, but it was also fascinating and rewarding: there was rarely a dull moment, though the stressful job exhausted us and probably reduced our life expectancy.

Because much of our work was confidential it was sometimes frustrating that even our colleagues had only a limited idea of the role we played and how we spent our coveted extra non-teaching time. This book sheds some light on the life of a guidance teacher and perhaps even helps to justify the need for teachers to take on that role. It may also do two other things: firstly, provide a glimpse of what it is like for youngsters who live in a deprived area trapped in the vicious circle of poverty and its attending evils; and secondly, enlist the compassion of some of us hitherto largely unaware of what life holds for those at the bottom of the social ladder.

Everything in the book did actually happen, though perhaps not always in the chronological order suggested. Every effort has been made to ensure no person featured is embarrassed by being recognisable and all names have been changed.

Chapter 1

Girl Goes to Court

A scruffy red head appeared round my door.

'Miss, kin Ah speak tae ye?'

'Of course.   Come in, Tracy,' I said, inwardly groaning as I pushed aside a huge pile of reports.

After hesitantly edging in the little thirteen-year-old seated herself on the chair beside my desk.   But, fidgeting with her chunky finger rings, she seemed unable to launch into conversation.

'What's bothering you?' I asked, after a pause.

'Well, it's my ma...'   she started and then tailed off.

1

Oh dear, I agonised internally, not another mother-teenager conflict!

'You're not getting on with her?' I prompted.

'No, it's no that! It's to do with my boyfriend... Ah don't know what to do!'

As her eyes watered I hastily offered a tissue.

'Your mother doesn't like him?' I assumed, trying to be helpful.

'No, no - she doesnae even ken him,' wailed the girl, by now in full flood.

I was confused. Tracy wasn't conforming to the normal pattern.

'Well, why don't you start at the beginning and tell me what's wrong?'

She blew her nose and started.

'Right. Ah've been seeing this boy Oopa -' She broke off, observing my puzzlement at the name. 'Short for Superman,' she explained, as if that made things clear.

'Yes, go on.' Teenagespeak was a familiar, if alien, language.

'Ah met him after he got oot o' reform school a month ago, an' we've been going ever since.' She snuffled into another paper hankie.

'So how does your mother come into this?'

Tracy looked embarrassed. 'Oopa took me tae the pictures last night, then walked me home. He's nineteen and really keen on me..... that's the problem,' she hiccupped.

'What do you mean?'

She hesitated and grabbed another tissue before taking a deep breath and launching in.

'He wanted to have sex wi' me,' she tumbled out. 'I wouldnae do it so he got mad wi' me. He says Ah've got tae show Ah really love him, and if Ah dinnae dae it he'll knife me!' Her voice rose to a wail as she lapsed into earnest poshspeak. 'What am I to do?'

This was truly more complicated than the usual my-mother-hates-me problem.

'Why not tell your mother, Tracy? She needs to know.'

'Ah cannae! She'd go tae the police! An' he says if anybody tells the police he'll knife them!' She sobbed hysterically.

I wryly pushed aside reflections on my own possible fate and pondered briefly.

'Tracy,' I said, 'don't worry. I'll deal with this. Tell nobody and don't let on why you were here today. If anyone asks you, here's your report card.' I unearthed it from the pile, thankful it was one of the few completed ones.

'What'll you do?' she asked doubtfully, bending the card between her fingers.

'I'll contact the police. He won't come after me,' I replied, sounding more confident than I felt. 'I'll let you know what happens, and when you can tell your mother.'

'Oh thanks Miss.' Her burden shared, she seemed relieved as she rose to go.

'And Tracy -'

'Yes?'

'Pop into the toilet as you go and give your face a wash.' Her mascara had riveted its way down her cheeks and she was a mess.

'Okay,' she grinned through her tears, almost cheerful as she left.

Clearly this was a police matter and I didn't delay in phoning our local community bobby. He promised to deal discreetly with Oopa who, not unexpectedly, was already known to him, and confident that he would cope, I returned to the writing of reports.

Swamped by a mass of other problems and duties over the next weeks, after telling Tracy what I'd done, I found it easy to dismiss Oopa from my mind, and our paths didn't cross for some time. So, months later, when I received a summons to appear as a witness at Court in a case against a 'Clark Kent' I was quite bewildered. The name seemed familiar, but the penny didn't drop till I called PC Macdonald and he reminded me about Oopa! Of course! Clark

Kent.....Superman ....Oopa...!   After laughing with him when it finally clicked, I asked what I could possibly contribute to a trial. He assured me my testimony that Tracy had been in real fear and distress was essential, and reluctantly I agreed to arrange to go to the trial. I was only too aware that things would pile up in my absence, and would be there on my return, my punishment for taking time off.

The day of the trial came: I waited endlessly in the witnesses' room, with no one to talk to and feeling like a fish out of water. I was thankful I'd brought a paperback with me - as I usually did when faced with long waits in hospitals and airports. Before resorting to it, I furtively took stock of some others in the room. Tracy was there, of course, nervously hunched beside a larger clone of herself, presumably her mother whom I had never met. They had been there some time, judging by the pile of sweet papers scattered on the floor beside them. Self-consciously we waved to each other across the room. Next to them a battle-worn social worker whom I'd once met at a Children's Hearing was slumped in a chair, rifling through dog-eared files.

In a corner a harassed woman tried to cope with pre-school twins, who were insistently climbing on the chairs and constantly falling off. We were all relieved when a kindly janitor pushed in through the door and dropped a box of plastic toys at her feet. 'Thank God for that,' she said. 'I never thought of bringing stuff from home!' Others shared her prayer.

As the noise lessened, I immersed myself in my detective story, thankfully anaesthetised to the passing of time.   Nothing happened for ages except a couple of interruptions when black-suited, important looking people came in for a quick word with someone, then left. I was heartened by the NO SMOKING notice, but, with the passing of time the inevitable fug developed, and I hadn't the nerve to open a window. The book worked its magic for an hour but I was gradually overtaken by increasing hunger and a nervousness I could no longer hold at bay.   I noticed others in the room fidgeting and wished I'd had the sense to bring a sandwich as some had.

Finally the door opened and a black-gowned being addressed us.

'Thank you for attending today,' he pronounced, in clipped tones.   'However your presence is no longer required as the accused has pleaded guilty. Please fill in your expenses form and hand it in at the desk as you leave.'

What an anticlimax! I was relieved but

disappointed, and I could tell by their expressions that the others too felt cheated of the drama in which they had expected to figure. As Tracy and her mother passed me, the older lady spoke.

'Thanks hen, for lookin' efter Tracy. Ah'm sorry there wasnae a trial but Ah hope that wee nyaff will get what's comin' tae him. Cheerio the now! Tracy, hold the door open for Miss!' And I passed through as, for once, a pupil let me go first.

Next morning a smiling Tracy paid me another visit. 'Ah just wanted tae thank ye for helping me and tae tell ye the court telt Oopa he had breached his probation and sent him back tae Polmont.'

'Oh thanks Tracy,' I said. 'I was wondering what had happened to him.'

'He'll no be botherin' me there!' she laughed and then held out a small gift-wrapped box. 'Take this - it's just a wee thank you present.'

An unexpected box of chocolates. Just the gift for a chocaholic! I thanked her warmly and, at her insistence, opened the gift. I did just manage to hide my disappointment when its contents were revealed - a box of tissues!

Chapter 2

Testing Tenting

It was almost lunchtime. Small wonder class 1L2 was flagging. Most of them would have had no breakfast. Having lost the girls' interest, I decided to change tack altogether.

'Put away your books', I called. 'All stand!'

'Not another quiz', someone groaned.

They loved quizzes, but appearing to enjoy school was not the done thing. They rose to their feet, already familiar with the rules: don't shout out answers, everyone must answer at least one question, sit down after answering one, win points for all answers after the first, and, finally, when the lunch bell rings everyone who has answered may go.

As one colleague had put it, 1L2 was 'one 'ell of a class'.   They all had mild learning problems and their ignorance was abysmal, but what they lacked in knowledge they made up for in personality, and I had a secret liking for them.

'First question.   Hands up!   Capital of Scotland?'

'Edinburgh!' yelled Jane, desperate to be first to sit down.

'Right, but you can't sit down - you didn't put up your hand.'

'Huh,' she muttered. 'That's no fair.' But she did remain standing.

'Next question.   A famous Scottish poet.' Four hands shot up, out of a possible seventeen.

'Mandy?'

'Robert Burns.'

'Very good!' Mandy slumped to her seat.

'Ready?   What do the letters UK stand for?' Two hands went up.

'Janice?'

'United Kingdom.'

'Good.   Now here's a hard one.' Groans. 'Spell Edinburgh.' Several girls raised their hands, jumping up and down enthusiastically because they were sure of the answer.

'Andrea?'

'Edwin died in November buried under –'

'Sorry, that's not the spelling. That's a way of remembering the spelling! Have another go.' But try as she might, without paper and pencil she was lost.

'Ah ken, Miss! Ask me, ask me!' urged Beth. Sure enough she knew it, and sat down with pride.

'Next question. A river starting with 'F'.'

Lizzie recalled 'Forth' and happily seated herself.

'The name of the Queen' got Angie off the hook.

No one standing knew a type of dog beginning with 'B', but Janice won a point with 'boxer'. I dredged up some things I'd repeatedly quizzed them on until only a few were left standing. It was had difficult to formulate questions easy enough for them. What could I be sure they would know?

Then the bell rang. All those sitting jumped to their feet to line up at the door. As I opened it, with a sense of achievement they poured out into the corridor, their next goal the dinner hall. I turned to face the remnant, mentally searching for quick easy questions.

'A shop in Princes Street?' Shona succeeded with this one and left.

'The name of our headmaster.' A relieved Carol knew that.

'The name of the sea out there?' Grace lisped 'Firth of Forth!' and departed beaming.

'What colour comes from mixing blue and yellow?' proved too hard, so I tried 'A Disney cartoon character,' and was glad when Jean came up with 'Donald Duck.'

Jackie the only one left, ended her captivity, and mine, by spelling 'postman', and so the lunch hour began.

As I locked up and made for the staffroom I couldn't help thinking about how much poverty limited their lives: confined to their deprived urban ghetto, they had money only for the basics, and not even that sometimes. Although they all had TV, most had no books in their homes. They went nowhere, and had no access to pursuits requiring equipment or entry fees. Most of them had never travelled by train and few had been outside Edinburgh. No wonder they had such a limited vocabulary, little imagination, and poor general knowledge. Laughter welled up inside me as I recalled the day I'd asked Jackie to name a mineral. She'd looked at me blankly, needing some help.

'Something you dig out of the ground,' I explained inadequately.

Light dawned. 'Wurrums!' she'd pronounced triumphantly, and only two of the class had had the

11

wit to laugh.

I wished I could do something to relieve the drabness of their lives. Just then I passed the Outdoor Store, and noticed some tents spread out to dry, and I had a mad idea. I could take 1L2 on a 24-hour camp!

These were innocent times. Child protection and risk aversion were not familiar terms in school. The Head and the girls' parents approved the trip, and so did the few staff who willingly sacrificed the privilege of teaching 1L2 for a morning. There was only a handful of girls in the class but they usually proved quite a handful!

Charging even a small fee would exclude some girls for money was always a problem. All of them had free school meals and since most of their families lived on meagre Social Security allowances the expedition had to be free. This was not a great problem as we planned to leave on a Friday and return next day at 10.00am. We'd only need three meals. Warned in advance, the school meals service would provide packed meals for those entitled to free food, so that left only two, a dinner and a breakfast, to arrange. Cooking facilities and the girls' diets were fairly limited, so we'd have to eat simply. After consultation, we agreed on the menus: for dinner tinned soup, sausages, beans and dried potato followed by tinned fruit and custard, and for breakfast bacon sandwiches.

Instead of asking for money, I Iisted each food needed and asked each girl to bring one specified item - custard, beans. margarine, bread and so on. This enlisted their participation and saved me a lot of work.   The School Fund's grant of £20 covered some necessary extras.

The day 'camp' was on a Friday because school closed early that day, and because I would have a two day recuperation period at the end.   Luckily we had free travel in the school bus and had access to tents, stoves, sleeping bags and all the necessary camping paraphernalia from the Outdoor Store.

As everyone else started classes on the Friday, 1L2 excitedly gathered at the outdoor store and, clacking like a bunch of noisy chickens, scurried around fussing over the equipment while we loaded up the van. Though I'd told them what few personal possessions they would need, some seemed to have come without anything.

'Where's your luggage?' I asked Shona, as she settled into her seat.

'Everythin's in ma pockets, Miss,' she replied, indicating her bulging left pocket from which protruded a packet of dried potato.

'But where's your towel and jammies?'   I

pursued.

'Oh ma mother said Ah wouldnae need them for jist one night.'

'Oh, right,' I said, slightly nonplussed. Even after years of working in poor housing schemes, my middle class expectations remained.   She probably had no pyjamas, and quite likely there was no towel to spare in her house, not to mention soap and toothpaste.

Only three of the class were missing.   Tracy's mother was having another baby and I was torn between delight and disappointment that the terrible twins, Linda and Lesley, were smitten with chicken pox.   All fourteen of the rest jammed into the Transit and we set off, cushioned by bulky tents and sleeping bags. We were only driving twelve miles to Musselburgh but it could have been Murmansk, for all the girls knew.   As I drove and they munched their way through endless supplies of sweets we had the inevitable quiz, with Jackie keeping the points.

'What's that building?'   I pointed to Fettes College.

'A hospital?' suggested Shona.

'No, it's a school,' said Grace dismissively.

'One point,' I said.   'Name the school for another.'

Mandy knew it was Fettes because her auntie was a cleaner there.

Incredibly, to some of them Princes Street was foreign territory. No one could put a name to the Scott Monument, and only two recognised Waverley Station.

'Remember these,' I warned. 'I'm going to ask you them on the way back.'

The quiz fizzled out at Abbeyhill because interest was waning and because no one seemed to have been beyond there. A delighted Shona won a Milky Way for gaining most points.

So far their behaviour had been exemplary but for one thing. I pulled in and parked briefly beyond Meadowbank stadium.

'Are we here?' asked Andrea.

'Dinnae be daft!' yelled Lizzie. 'This is only Meadowbank - ma Dad lives over there.'

'Quiet!' I shouted. 'Now I didn't remind you of the minibus rules but I'm going to do that now. No standing up, no waving to people, and no throwing rubbish out of the windows!'

'But we havnae,' protested a voice. 'We've been good.'

'Maybe you have,' I said, 'but in my mirror I've just seen two of you waving and making rude signs! Jean and Jackie!'

'Oh Miss,' said the mendacious Jean, 'we were jist wavin' tae ma uncle in that car.'

I ignored the excuse. 'No waving's allowed,' I said fiercely,' even if it's your grannie, you mother or your very best friend! Don't give me a red face!'

'Sorry, Miss,' said Jackie hurriedly. She had once been ejected from a minibus and given her bus fare home.

That settled, we continued and, after twenty uneventful minutes, arrived at Carberry. Mercifully it was dry and the weather seemed settled. The girls were impressed, even awed, when they saw the house and grounds.

'This belonged tae the Queen's cousin, didn't it, Miss,' pronounced Grace.

'Yes. She left it to the Church of Scotland. Look! See that green space amongst the trees? That's where we're camping! We'll drive round and I'll show you the toilets behind the house.'

'Miss, our camp's miles frae the toilets,' protested Jean. 'Ah'm no gaun there in the middle o' the night!' Everyone giggled.

'Go behind a tree,' I suggested. 'It'll be dark and nobody will see you.'

'Pee outside!' she said incredulously. 'What if an animal gets me?'

Their knowledge of wildlife was not extensive.

'You'll be quite safe,' I reassured her, well aware that these noisy human animals would scatter all innocent creatures for miles around.

'We've got a torch for every tent,' I revealed, and that kept them happy meantime.

Having parked close to the campsite, we all set to, milling about, unpacking and looking for flat ground. The class had already had instruction in pitching tents from the Outdoor Education instructor so were eager to start . After indicating the circle along whose perimeter the tents would be pitched, I left them to it while I erected my own trusted Vango Force 10 and flung myself down on my sleeping bag for a short breather.

It was just noon by the time the camp was set up. When I emerged the tents were not too awry and the campers were enjoying the novelty of crawling in and out, inspecting each other's work. As I watched them unpack their minimal luggage from their plastic Tesco and Co-op bags, I saw Jean pull out a packet of margarine, her food contribution. Disgusted to find it squashed, she tossed it over her shoulder into the trees.

'Jean, we need that!' I called.

'But it's disgusting!'

'No it's not, and we haven't any more!'

'Well Ah'm no eatin' it,' she announced.   But with an ill grace she did retrieve it for the rest of us to use.

'Miss, Ah'm starving,' said Shona. 'Can we eat now?'

'Naw, can we no explore first?' suggested Beth.

I knew few would have eaten breakfast, though they had consumed quantities of sweets on the journey. 'We'll eat now,' I conceded. 'Let's get together on the big tarpaulin.'

And thus we had our first al fresco meal, by courtesy of 'School Dinners'.

'This is great. Ah've only ever picnicked in the back green,' said one.

'Oh in good weather my ma sometimes takes us tae Silverknowes,' said Beth.

The picnic disappeared fast, but when we rose to clear up I found we were encircled by a ring of discarded apple cores, crisp packets and clingfilm.

'Hey,' I yelled at their disappearing backs,' we need to pick up all this litter!'

Grimacing in protest, they trailed back to retrieve what they'd discarded.

'The queen's cousin's house is not a dump,' I nagged. 'When we leave, nobody's to be able to know we've been here!'

'How come? The grass is dead flat already,' Lizzie protested.

It'll jump right up once we go,' I assured her. 'Now, you have thirty minutes to explore, before we go to the beach. Stay in twos, don't leave the grounds, and keep away from the house and the pond. Right?'

'Right!' and they scuttled off, determined to make the most of their free time. Meanwhile, I retired to my Vango to top up my caffeine levels and scan my newspaper. When I blew my whistle half an hour later half of them emerged from their tents and several others reluctantly abandoned the huge copper beech they'd been climbing. Angie proffered a large bunch of wild campions, stitchwort and hyacinths.

'Look, Miss, Ah brought ye these,' she smiled.

'Oh Angie, you're not supposed to pick wild flowers,' I protested.

'Yeah, Mr. Bell telt us that, but there was hundreds! They'll never miss them!'

It was a kind thought, but don't pick more or we'll be in trouble.' I discreetly put them inside my tent. It was still only two o'clock. Never had a day passed so slowly.

'When are we gaun tae the beach?' asked Carol.

'Now,' was my reply. 'Bring your wellies and cagoules. Zip up your tents before you go.'

Our trip to Gullane beach was an eye-opener for girls who'd been no further than Cramond.

It's huge!' yelled Carol. 'Ah wish Ah had a camera.'

We straggled through the dunes carrying cagoules

and games equipment.

'Can we swim?' asked Andrea, enticed by the bright sun and sands. 'Please, Miss,' she appealed.

'No. It's too cold and we've no swimsuits. But we can paddle,' I suggested, pulling off my shoes.

We dropped everything and made for the water.

'Aw, it's freezing!' screamed Andrea, running out at speed.

'A Milky Way to anyone who goes in up to their knees!' I called out.

This provided motivation and I was glad I'd brought a whole boxful. Only the two who determinedly 'paddled' in their wellies were denied the reward. The tide was out and we played rounders, French cricket and dodge ball...till everyone had dropped out to make castles and sand pies. Simple things gave them so much pleasure. I'd taken squash and biscuits for a surprise snack and after that we resorted to the deep sand bowl at the eastern end of the sands. There they played like puppies, rolling down the dunes, or, more daringly, jumping off the top.

At last, hunger combined with a slight sand storm demanded a return to Carberry, and we made our way back to the car park despite several protests that it was too soon. I turned a blind eye to the sand that was going to have to be swept out of the van and we headed back.

Luckily the fair weather continued and back at Carberry we had no need to rig up a cooking shelter. Grace helpfully held up an end of the tarpaulin to shield the Gaz stoves from the wind and, with no shortage of competent cooks, water was boiled and everything cooked in double quick time. I was amused at how quickly they adapted to roughing it: when Jean dropped a couple of sausages in the grass she unceremoniously wiped them and placed them in the pan.

It was 7.30pm by the time we'd eaten. How slowly time was passing! But the minutiae of camping is generally time consuming and not till 9pm was everything tidied away. Darkness was falling and there was a noticeable reluctance in the girls to leave the camping circle.

'There's nae lights,' complained Lizzie. 'How are we tae get washed?'

'Ah'm no washin' till Ah get hame,' muttered Grace, but I ignored this.

'Let's get the torches and we'll all go over together,' I suggested. Bunched together, with even Grace in our midst, unwilling to be left alone, we stumbled across to the back of the house.

'Thank Gawd for the electric!' trilled Lizzie as she switched on the washroom lights.

'Aye!' chorused the rest, elbowing past her into the light. They didn't do much washing but it was hard to winkle them out of the light and back into the darkness. Eventually, clinging to each other and screaming at every shadow, they left en masse and I saw them into their tents before I returned to wash in private.

'Oh no!' I said to myself as, entering the toilets, I caught the faint whiff of tobacco. I shot back to the camp half expecting to see the tents in flames but nothing seemed amiss apart from some shrieks, and shadowy figures silhouetted against the canvas. Deviously I started a second round of 'goodnights' and my sharp nose detected the possible culprits in Tent 3.

'Jane and Mandy, you've been smoking!' I exclaimed angrily. 'Naked lights in tents are strictly forbidden!'

'Aw, no Miss,' said Mandy, 'we didnae smoke a fag in here. We jist had a wee puff in the toilets.'

'Hand over the cigarettes!' I demanded, and the two shame-faced girls produced one and a bit crumpled cigarettes and three matches. 'Is that the lot?'

They nodded.

'And you Jane, could bring cigarettes but couldn't afford a decent sized tin of beans!'

Tears welled up in Jane's eyes. 'Ma mother had nae money, Miss.'

I knew it was probably true, and felt bad. 'Where did the cigarettes come from, then?'

'Ah nicked two from her bag. Oh Miss, dinnae tell her or she'll batter me!'

That was likely too, and I decided their punishment would be more constructive. 'You've broken my rules, so I'll decide your punishment. Tomorrow you'll both get up early and thoroughly clean all the toilets and washbasins, and when we're all ready to leave you'll gather up every single scrap of rubbish and put it in the bins! Understand?'

'Yes Miss,' they muttered repentantly.

Following this, the atmosphere was chilly for a time, but my hope of getting a little sleep was soon squashed. Their spirits soon revived, their efforts at entertaining each other with jokes and ghost stories evoked wild shrieks and laughter, and vainly I plugged in my earphones and turned up the radio volume. Eventually I collapsed into sleep about 2am, only to dream of being chased across wild Arctic wastes by howling wolves - a dream no doubt inspired by the cold, and the campers' noises off.

The night ended when the first girl woke at 5am: loud whispers enquiring if her friends were awake soon ensured that they were. Rising briefly, I entreated them to go for a quiet walk without waking the neighbourhood, and soon, after much zooping of tent zips and subdued giggling, an apparent herd of them thundered off in the direction of the woods.

Further sleep eluded me till their return at 6.30am when I decided I'd better rise and start my day. As the tents were wet with dew we left them up till after breakfast to let them dry. The school wellies and the big tarpaulin were a boon in the long wet grass.

For breakfast we wolfed down our bacon sandwiches, supplemented by bread and jam, and hot tea - more than most of us usually had, but the cold fresh air sharpened our appetites.

Spontaneously Jean and Mandy, without any reminding, did their punishment duty in the washroom and toilets while the rest of us struck camp, and by the time they returned the site was ready for their scavenging.

I heard Mandy surreptitiously mimic 'The queen's cousin's house is not a dump!' as she and Jean laughingly did the needful, depositing discarded soggy wrappers and other detritus in black bin bags.

'Miss, can we no stay till the morn?' pleaded Carol.

'Naw, let's stay here till Sunday!' suggested Janice.

'But there's nae food left,' objected Shona, 'an'

Ah've got ma paper job the night.'

'Don't worry,' I reassured her. 'We are going home, right now!' and, suiting my action to these words, I climbed into the driving seat of the van and waited for my reluctant class to join me.

'Can we come back next weekend?' asked Angie.

'Aye,' beamed the undaunted Jean and Mandy, in chorus.

I felt weak at the thought. 'Not next weekend,' was my answer, 'but maybe later on...'

Cheered by what they took as a promise they boarded the bus; but I resolutely put the whole idea out of my mind meanwhile, until I recovered, if ever.

Chapter 3

The Unexpected

'Billie!' A trusted colleague tapped me on the shoulder. 'I've heard something you should know about.'

'Oh, what's that?' My curiosity was aroused as we continued along the corridor.

'Word is circulating in the staffroom that Janice Livingstone may be pregnant,' she said quietly. 'One of the PE staff says she's gaining weight fast.'

I was shocked that a member of staff could act so unprofessionally, but I put that aside for the moment. 'That's impossible! She can't be,' I protested. 'I know she used to be a tearaway, but she's settled down in the last few months and her work's been steadily improving.'

'Well, it's probably only a rumour, but I thought you ought to hear it,' said Meg, as she turned into her classroom.

In spite of my denials my heart was sinking as I reached the office. I really didn't believe this story but I couldn't let it lie. I had to take action, but what? I could hardly ask the girl outright - the very thought brought me out in a cold sweat. I imagined visions of a shocked student...irate parents... a furious Headteacher... headlines in the Mail... and the end of my guidance career.

While I pondered the problem, deep in thought, I heard a knock on the door and fervently wished for a brief moment of uninterrupted peace. 'Come in,' I called, hoping whoever it was could be dealt with fast.

In came Iris, a likeable fourth year girl, whose work and behaviour left nothing to be desired.

'Hello, Iris. Can I help you with something?' I asked, resigned to putting aside my problem for the moment.

'Well, yes. At least I think so,' she faltered, taking the seat across from me.

'Nothing wrong, I hope? Your report card was excellent.'

'Thanks. No, it's not about anything like that,' she hesitated. 'It's to do with Janice.'

My heart skipped a beat. Outwardly impassive, I braced myself for some unpalatable news. 'Janice?'

'Janice Livingstone, you know. She's in my tutor group and we pal about together.'

'Oh yes.'

'I feel terrible - I don't know how to tell you this-' She hesitated, searching for words.

'Go on,' I encouraged her, pretty sure of what was coming. Iris was well enough acquainted with me to know I would accept any revelation calmly, without a scene.

'I think she's pregnant.' It tumbled out.

Just what I was expecting but didn't want to hear. 'You must be pretty sure before you would say that,' I responded.

Iris had two bright spots of pink on her cheeks. 'She told me her periods have stopped, and she's put on a lot of weight. She's quite worried...' she tailed off, visibly trembling. 'She'll kill me for telling you, but -'

'Iris,' I interrupted, 'you've had the courage to do

exactly the right thing.   She will not kill you - I'm certain she'll be relieved and really pleased you did this!'

'But Miss,' Iris interjected, 'what if she's not pregnant?'

'In that case, Iris, we'll all breathe sighs of relief and take on board a few lessons!'

Pregnant fifteen year olds were a rarity in the seventies, and I'd had no experience of them. Confronting Janice wasn't going to be easy, but at least I now had some grounds for doing so.   After lunch, when I had a stretch of free time, I phoned to ask her history teacher to ask if Janice might come down.

As we met, it would be hard to say which of us was more nervous, although both of us were outwardly calm. 'Janice,' I asked, 'have you any idea why I might want to see you?'

'No Miss.'

I didn't expect a different reply.   I had rehearsed what I might say, but saying it was another thing. 'Well I realise you have put on a lot of weight recently and I wondered if there was a reason for that.'

'No Miss.'   She gave her stock reply, but did look slightly less composed.

My heart went out to her.   Would she ever find

herself in a worse situation? I decided to cut short the agony and take the plunge. 'Do you think you might be pregnant?' I asked her quietly, though it felt as if the question was resounding round the room.

'I don't think so.' Her head was down and she clasped her hands together.

I gently persisted, in the face of her denial. 'Well Janice, you are the only person who can say whether there is the slightest possibility that you might be. Is it absolutely impossible, or is there a slim chance you are?'

'It could maybe be true,' she almost whispered.

'Would it not be better to be certain one way or another?' I suggested.

'Yes,' she croaked, and then said more forcefully, 'but I can't tell my mother!'

'We'll face that if we need to. How would you like to have a chat with the school doctor? I could arrange for you to see her when she comes tomorrow.'

She breathed out heavily. 'Yes, I could do that.'

Poor girl. I was almost as much in denial as she was, and I shared her hope that this was a false alarm. Neither of us gave voice to the similar scenarios we were both anticipating if she really was expecting a child.

'I hope you don't object to my asking about this,'

I said as she rose to leave. 'Try not to worry too much - it could be a false alarm.' Platitudes! But I'd had no practice and words were failing me.

'Right, Miss. Thanks. See you tomorrow.' Her usual jauntiness had abandoned her but she walked out of the room looking more in command of the situation than I felt myself to be.

The school doctor and the nurse were the only appropriate people with whom I could share this in the meantime, and I made contact without delay, glad that they were scheduled to be in school for the following morning. After spending the afternoon doing desultory tasks, unable to concentrate, I left for home and a restless night.

I was mightily relieved to see Janice at my door as classes were about to begin. My overnight fears of her absconding, truanting or even harming herself were happily unfounded. I explained that she had the first appointment with the doctor and, shaking, I think, almost as much as she was, took her to the medical room where she was sympathetically received.

As I waited the doctor's verdict, I buried myself in requisitions for Social Education, another of my responsibilities, and started thumbing through catalogues on personal development and careers education. Fortunately, my wait was not prolonged.

Within half an hour the nurse appeared at the door with Janice. From their demeanour the news was clear before they voiced it. Janice was seven months pregnant! There was no question of a termination. The doctor would deal with Janice's parents, who had rarely made contact with the school; my job would be to cope with the educational fall-out.

The Headteacher had to know, of course, but it was not appropriate to spread this confidence around the staff. Apart from stating she could not remain in school, he gave me carte blanche to make what arrangements were necessary for her education and asked to be kept informed.

I did tell Meg, my very discreet colleague, knowing it would go no further. She met me just after I'd heard the news and noticed my pallor.

'You look awful - are you feeling okay?' she asked. She was the one person I occasionally confided in, and I felt I owed it to her on this occasion to tell her what was wrong. Her reply was quite refreshing.

'For goodness' sake, Billie,' she said, 'it's not the end of the world! Pull yourself together! It's not you that's pregnant!'

I laughed ruefully, and reminded myself yet again that counsellors had to stand back and not become emotionally involved with their clients. Some cases did take their toll, though.

Now that it was certain Janice was pregnant, I had to confront the two young PE teachers who had been discussing the possibility with their friends in the staffroom. I bearded them in their den, so to speak, the PE office. I was angry that they had deduced her condition because of their professional dealings with her in the gym, but had not had the professionalism to report their suspicions to the guidance staff. I pointed this out to them but excused them on the grounds of their inexperience and youth. I did however make it plain that they had failed in their duty to this student and that I would expect them to know better if another such occasion ever arose. They were suitably penitent and at the end of the interview we parted on reasonably good terms.

As I was clearly out of my depth as to how to proceed with Janice, I consulted Pauline, a good friend and a social worker, who was aware of what resources were on offer. She suggested Janice should consult the Guild of Service, a voluntary organisation for families in need. They would discuss the options with Janice and her parents and give any necessary practical help. I was glad to hear they would also bring into the equation the young father, someone who had played as large a part as she had in bringing about this predicament.

In the event, Janice, in spite of all the circumstances weighted against her, decided not to have her baby adopted and determined to bring it up herself. Amazingly, Janice's parents, unable to handle the situation, washed their hands of her, upped sticks, and left to live almost as far away as possible, in Bristol. Perhaps this apparent callousness explained why none of their children had ever been a model student. Nevertheless, fifteen-year-old Janice coped magnificently, maybe because she was used to being self-directing. Her social worker arranged for a supportive family to give her a tiny attic flat and care for her, in return for which she did some ironing and baby-sitting.

Educationally, there were some problems. Janice was not eligible to leave school for another six months and, an able girl, she had been entered for seven SCE 'O' Grade exams which were only three months away. She was obliged to have lessons until she reached the leaving age. Fortunately, I was able to arrange for the Education Department to provide home tuition for her on health grounds. Janice was apparently not much phased by all that was going on around her. On the contrary, she was highly motivated and studied hard to do well in her exams so that she might gain entrance to a career which would help her provide for her baby. Since she had no family support, I encouraged her school friends to keep up with her, and, as she was based close to where I was living it was easy for me to drop in on her from time to time.

It was no time at all before Janice was admitted to the maternity hospital: she was taken in early because of her youth and some minor health problems. Happily, before being hospitalised she had been able to sit all her exams except chemistry. She intended to train as a lab. technician and this was her main subject. However all was not lost. Sitting up in bed a few days before giving birth, she determinedly applied herself to her chemistry exam - and later found she had deservingly passed with flying colours.

The Guild of Service did a magnificent job for Janice, seeing that she received welfare benefits, and providing supportive accommodation for her and her little boy till she was able to have her own tenancy. But Janice showed outstanding character, too. I was in irregular contact with her for some time, and found her daily routine involved rising before seven each morning, taking the boy to a day nursery, going to work or college, and returning to pick up the baby at five in the evening. A very young single mother, she achieved her ambition, studying and qualifying as a lab. technician while caring for her child on her own. If only maternity conferred that sense of determination and responsibility on all schoolgirl mothers!

Eventually we lost touch, but several years later I was delighted to receive a letter which I still treasure. She told me she was happily married to a lovely man with whom she'd had two children and who had received Sean as his own. Clearly, life was what she had made it.

This story contrasts with that of another pregnant schoolgirl I encountered later. She too was in Fourth Year and about to sit her SCE exams, but it was her mother who brought her in to break the news.

'I'm sorry to say Margaret's pregnant,' she confided, her fingers shaking as she pulled her chair up to my desk. Her father's broken-hearted,' she said, 'and we don't know what to do next.'

Margaret, though pale and composed, was clearly upset.

I did try to reassure them that it wasn't the end of the world, but this was not the time for that. What they needed right now was practical advice and action. Having established Margaret's baby was due in four months, I suggested they should approach the Guild of Service for support, and explained what the organisation had to offer. Both mother and daughter agreed to a referral and I telephoned there and then to get them an appointment for the next day.

Our Headmaster, proud of the comprehensive sex education programme we had established in the school and jealous for the school's reputation, reacted with typical male intolerance.

'Tell her to have a termination.'

'It's not just as easy as that,' I protested.

'She's too young, just starting out on life!'

'I know. But she has to make her own decision. It's her life, and her child.'

'We can't have her in school if she keeps the baby - for health and safety reasons if for nothing else,' he pronounced.

'I know. We'll probably get her home tuition,' I replied.

'Hmm, right. Well keep me up to scratch,' he instructed me, and I assented to this, but I quietly resolved to keep my revelations to the minimum, discretion being essential.

In due time Margaret told me she was planning to have the baby adopted: the father was in agreement. Only her tutor, and the few teachers who would provide teaching materials for her and enter her for exams, were discreetly informed and asked to let the matter go no further. Knowing staffrooms, I expect it did go further, although I was not thereafter aware of any gossip.

Margaret was planning a career in office work and it was reasonably easy to find home tutors for English, Maths, and History, but not for Shorthand, Typing or Accounting.   However, a good friend of mine who lectured in these subjects was easily prevailed upon to do a few months' home tuition in the evenings; competent and sympathetic, she was ideal for the post.   Thus, Margaret became a long row of zeros on the school register till we could officially record her as a school leaver, and she soon lost touch with us on entering the adult world.

It was about fifteen years later when we next met up, at a school jubilee reunion.   I did not at first recognise this confident and elegant lady who approached me. 'I just wanted to thank you for what you did for me all those years ago,' she said, smiling.

My mind went into overdrive.   'What had I done? Careers help? Help when bullied? Duke of Edinburgh Award? Domestic violence?'

She provided a clue. 'I thought you'd be interested to know David and I got married in the end, and we now have two more children.'

Of course, it was Margaret! She and David had parted after the baby's birth and gone their separate ways after the trauma of the adoption, but when they met up again as mature adults they found the chemistry that had initially attracted them to each other these years ago was still there, and they had been happily married for quite a few years. Happily married except for one thing: the sadness of being the parents of an adopted child, their two children's full sibling, with whom they had no contact.

'But,' said Margaret, 'we were too young. We could never have coped.' Her eyes watered a little. 'We did the right thing at the time.'

'You did,' I agreed. And I truly believe they did, but I never think of Margaret now without a sense of sadness and feeling a little tearful for her myself.

Chapter 4

Surprise Ending

'Over to you!' I gasped as I reeled into the staffroom and collapsed into a chair exhausted.

'Oh it's not as bad as all that!' laughed Rob, who along with me and one or two others had drawn the short straw and been forced to do duty at the fifth year Christmas disco.

'Well, maybe you enjoy repelling strangers at the

windows and policing the toilets, but it's not my idea of how to spend a Friday night!' I complained.

'I got the janitors to smell the kids' breath as they came in,' said Rob, 'but no one seemed to have been drinking.'

'Don't be too sure! Last year Dougie Hanson smuggled vodka through in a coke bottle and they had a secret booze up at the bottom of C block,' I warned him, as he left to start his patrol.

I made a coffee and slumped down in my chair, relieved to have briefly avoided the decibels of the disco, but resenting how slowly my two hour stint was passing. When my eye fell on a magazine on the coffee table I picked it up; it was only an EIS Magazine, the journal of the teachers' union, but for want of anything better I started reading. An English Speaking Union advert for the 'Walter Hines Page Travelling Scholarship' drew my attention and I read on with interest. It offered a month's travel in the USA making visits investigating an educational project which would enhance the applicant's professional development. This was worth a second thought. At that moment I would have done almost anything to escape from a school where in my first six years I had felt a misfit: the prospect of escaping for even one month was enticing. As I finished my coffee and rose to return to the front line, I was thoughtful.

I made my way towards the girls' toilets. I noticed that the two six-footers from the technical department, backing up the janitors at the front door, had been relieved by two other colleagues, shorter in stature but equally strong armed. A crate containing various bottles, some half empty, lay behind them and Wally, the head janitor, was delivering a warning to a belligerent senior whose bottle had just been confiscated.

'Well Ah don't care what it cost – you cannae have it back! You're under age. Ah'll gi'e it tae yer Dad if he comes round for it,' he offered, knowing full well that was a most unlikely scenario.

Reflecting grimly on the Friday night example Mr Hanson was probably setting his son right then, I strode on, eager to get my duty over. This comprised throwing open the toilet door and persuading the dozen or so girls gathered there to go and enjoy the evening in a more salubrious place. Then, still denying my sense of smell, I had to inspect each cubicle and cistern for any sign of drink or drugs. That done, I took a roundabout pathway through the assembly hall towards the disco and cruelly spoilt love's young dream for two couples having a quiet snog.

Just as I was bracing myself to re-enter the dark and deafening disco I spotted H.A. who had arrived early to relieve me and start his tour of duty. True, I had 'done' detention for him that Friday afternoon, but had been somewhat sceptical of his promise to 'do extra time tonight'. After giving him a quick progress report I made haste to leave, stopping only to borrow the EIS Journal from the staffroom.

I realised I had less than a week to register my interest in applying, and it was mandatory to send a reference from my headmaster along with a character reference. That weekend I completed my application: my project would be 'Guidance and Counselling in Areas of Urban Deprivation'. To be sure of meeting the deadline, I mailed it on the Monday morning to the English Speaking Union with the promise of references to follow. Before long I revealed my intentions to the Head. For me to be away for a month would cause some inconvenience, I knew, but useful ideas I picked up in the course of my travels could prove very valuable to the school and widen our vision.

'There's a month's travelling scholarship advertised in the current EIS Journal and I thought I'd apply for it,' I explained, dreading his inevitable cynicism. 'I'd be grateful if you could give me a reference'.

Luckily he was busy, and he showed little interest. 'Hmm, yes,' he hesitated. 'just jot down for me one or two things I should say....'

As I left I felt somewhat confused. 'How could I write my own reference? Was that what he wanted?' I thought as I left his study. 'He knows I am a good disciplinarian, never ill, late or absent. He's well aware of the Wednesday evening club and the residential trips I run. I can hardly blow my own trumpet and explain how conscientious, reliable, and co-operative I am......'

Unwilling to put words in his mouth, so to speak, I delayed doing anything, but went back a few days later to repeat my request for a reference.

He made the same reply. 'Just write down what I should say.'

In the end I provided him with a list of extra-curricular activities I'd been involved in of which he might be unaware: I'd lectured at Napier College on guidance to careers officers training, been asked to write an article on guidance for the Inspectors' Bulletin, led various seminars at Edinburgh in-service training days, and had articles published in The Scotsman and Times Educational Supplement.

I was appalled when he handed me the reference next day. He had replicated verbatim exactly what I had given him, only adding 'All this testifies to Miss Smith's interest in furthering her career in Guidance.' He had contrived to be totally neutral and written nothing whatsoever about me as a person or as a professional!

This was useless but what could I do, especially when time was so short. However, I did spend a third of my time teaching English and in desperation I decided to ask the principal teacher of English for a reference. The resulting document also proved embarrassingly inappropriate: it comprised four closely handwritten pages, extolling me as possessing every possible virtue as a colleague, and as an English teacher, ending with 'the child who is taught by Miss Smith is indeed fortunate.'

My close friend's reaction was predictable. 'You can't possibly send this! You're more angelic than the angels!' she said. ' It's absolutely fulsome!'

'What on earth am I to do?' I asked despairingly. In the end, all expectation dashed, I just sent both documents and left the ESU officials to make of them what they could.

Three weeks later I was surprised and delighted to be summoned for an interview and, following that, really thrilled when I was informed my application for the Walter Hines Page Scholarship had been successful. I would have four weeks away, all expenses paid, travelling extensively in the USA. Although members of the English Speaking Union would host me I was invited to name friends of my own who would accommodate me, and I had the freedom to include in my itinerary any places I wanted to visit.

So it was that in my fortieth year I had the privilege of crossing the Atlantic for the first time and travelling through a dozen states from east to west in the U. S. As well as visiting over twenty widely varied educational establishments I was able to savour the delights of the Grand Canyon and Niagara Falls, and had the pleasure of meeting many American colleagues and making many new friends, some of them professionals and some of them families providing hospitality.

The adage 'Life begins at forty' was certainly fulfilled, for this whole experience proved very refreshing; furthermore, after the retiral of the previous Head just after my return, I found myself catapulted into a welcome new regime where I was much happier and more professionally fulfilled.

N.B. An official report of the scholarship tour can be found in Appendix C at the end of the book.

Chapter 5

A Tangled Web

Gill, one of the housemistresses, called me from her house office to ask for some advice, so I invited her down for a cup of coffee. 'You know Billy Davidson?' she asked.

'The Fourth Year boy who's never here?'

'Yes. Well I was interviewing him yesterday afternoon. I'm very worried about him and his brother.'

'Alex? But he attends and behaves OK,' I replied.

'Yes. But the situation's very complicated. What really set me thinking was that Billy told me Alex spends every weekend in Portobello with an uncle who's a retired lawyer.'

'A real uncle?' I asked, aware that it was very unlikely a lawyer was related to this poverty stricken family living on benefits.

'Ah, no. He just calls him uncle. He's a friend of Alex's stepfather.'

'Oh. So what's the problem?'

'The whole thing is very iffy. 'Uncle' buys Alex loads of clothes, and showers him with presents. Last week he got a new bike. And they're going on holiday together.'

'Have you spoken to Alex about this?'

'Yes, the subject came up this morning when he brought me his field trip form. I was so surprised he was able to pay the full amount – he's only ever paid five pounds before. But 'uncle' is paying for it!'

'Did he say anything else about 'uncle'?'

'No. Only that he's not a real uncle but someone his stepfather drinks with in the pub.'

'Oh dear.' Gill was right. The set-up was very questionable.

'And I'm also concerned about Billy himself.'

'Why's that?'

'You know Mrs. Price, the boys' mother?'

'I've met her, yes. A poor timid little woman.'

'According to Billy, she's petrified of her husband.

48

He seems to be a violent bully and a layabout, who beats her up. She doesn't sleep with him but sits up all night in an armchair in the living room. He treats her like dirt and Billy hates him, passionately.'

'Is that why he's off so much?'

'Yes. He's trying to protect his mother from him. But Billy's terrified of him as well. This is a real can of worms. My gut feeling is there's a lot more to this. I tentatively asked him if there was a sexual element.'

'How did he react?'

'Believe it or not, he actually started to cry. He's at his wits' end and a whole lot of stuff poured out. You know Lucy Cameron?'

'In Second Year? What's she got to do with this?'

'Nothing, I hope. But she and her mother and a ten-year-old sister live in the flat above the Prices. Only, the little sister, Connie, sleeps downstairs every night in the Prices' house.'

'Never!'

'Yes, really! When I asked Billy about the sleeping arrangements, he told me he and Alex share a room and John Price sleeps in the other bedroom with Connie and his own nine-year- old boy, in two single beds tied together!'

'Are you sure of this?'

'Billy's not lying! I asked if John Price had ever

49

sexually molested Billy himself and it was clear he had.'

'Oh God, no,' I prayed. I felt quite sick at what Gill had unearthed.

'He also said his stepfather had porno pictures propped along the mantelpiece –'

'Why doesn't Mrs. Price do something about all this!'

'She's helpless. He beats her up! She can't! But what are we going to do?'

The issues here were immense, and urgent. 'Does Billy know you are taking this further?'

'Yes. I told him the police and Social Work would have to be involved.'

'How did he react?'

'I think he was pleased something would be done. But he's scared out of his wits because he's grassed.'

'With good reason. That man is dangerous.'

'He knows. I told him to keep his mouth shut at all costs.'

'Where's Billy now?'

'He's in the learning centre – supposedly working on a project.'

'Keep an eye on him. I'll approach Social Work first, and we'll take things from there.'

'Right. I'll go and help him with his project and see that he's OK.'

'Fine. I'll keep you informed.'

Speed was of the essence. Unwilling to be delayed or overheard, I made sure a senior social worker, Gary Millan, was available and went in person to the nearby Social Work Office to talk to him.

Amazingly, none of the families involved was known in the Department, and we had only Billy's word to go on. A phone call by Gary to the police, however, established they already had suspicions about the 'uncle' in Portobello, so we decided our concerns for the children were justified, and arranged an urgent case conference for the next afternoon.

There was no saying what his violent stepfather might do if he knew he was about to be exposed and, though we knew events were proceeding as fast as we could expect, we were in great trepidation regarding the boys' safety. Gill briefed Billy and warned him to go home as normal and behave as if nothing had happened, and we too went to our respective homes nursing horrible secrets and wishing tomorrow would come immediately.

After a sleepless night, I spent the next morning getting up to date on the boys' attendance, behaviour, attainments and other details. In addition, without divulging the reasons, I had an enlightening chat with Lucy Cameron's tutor wondering if her behaviour could throw any light on what was happening, but the morning dragged on and this day was one of the few in my guidance career when I was unable to face lunch. Gill felt the same.

Quite a formidable group of people attended the case conference in the Social Work Offices: the school doctor and nurse, Connie's class teacher and headmistress, Gill and I, two police representatives, and Gary and another social worker. Although none of the families had a history of social work involvement, as we shared information the picture that took shape was horrifying. The 'uncle' in Portobello had already been drawn to the attention of the police by a neighbour, concerned about the number of young boys frequenting his house, but, without proof of wrongdoing, the police had been unable to proceed against him. Connie, said her teacher, had recently appeared in a new pair of shoes, paid for, she said, by 'John', a neighbour who was friendly with her mother. Connie had not mentioned her sleeping arrangements but she had said John was very good to her mother and gave her £10 a week to 'help her out'. There was a sharp indraw of breath from the policewoman present.

'We've suspected Mrs. Cameron was into prostitution, but this is something else!'

Attention swung to Lucy Cameron when I reported that she was doing well academically, but that her tutor was puzzled by the detailed and convincing stories she constantly wove for her classmates about the pony she owned and stabled in Queensferry and rode every weekend.

'She's a really bright girl,' I observed, 'and she has everyone believing her!   In fact, I almost think she believes it herself.'

'Pure fantasy,' said the doctor.   'Poor kid.   Real life is so awful she can't face it and she's invented an alternative life for herself...'

After we shared what we had heard from Billy, everyone was unanimous on the need for immediate action. The police doubted whether John Price could be held in custody for long until they had hard evidence against him, but they would pull him in for questioning, and this would provide a window of opportunity for Gary and his colleagues to see to the needs of the boys and their mother.   Mrs Cameron would be seen that evening, if possible.

Mrs Price, when approached, was at the end of her tether and jumped at the prospect of going to a Women's Refuge where she would be safe from her violent husband.   She was concerned that only the youngest boy, Roddy, would be of age to be there with her but accepted that Billy and David would be safe in emergency foster care till she could, with help, take over Price's tenancy of the house and return home with all three boys.

Gary reported to me that Mrs. Cameron, when interviewed, at least feigned shock when she heard John Price was being held by the police, and, predictably, denied any collusion with him, protesting her concern for her children's welfare. Neither the police nor the social workers was in a position to proceed against her but both hoped that their interest in, and involvement with, the girls, would protect them against any further exposure to the sexual predation they believed had occurred, but which the whole family denied.

John Price was rigorously grilled by the police but of course denied everything. On the evidence of Billy and his mother he was charged with sexually assaulting a minor, and with lewd and libidinous conduct but he was represented by an extremely competent lawyer who procured a fairly lenient sentence.

Mrs. Price, who, it turned out, was the legal tenant of the house, was given assistance to have her husband excluded from the family home and barred from communicating with the family; once it became clear that she and her three boys were truly rid of him, she had the courage to return home and take charge of the family. Alex's trips to Portobello ceased, and Gary arranged for the boys to have regular informal social work supervision.

Everyone in school was mercifully unaware of the events in this saga as they unfolded, but that did mean that, as ever, the guidance staff were unable to defend themselves against the jibes of their unappreciative colleagues.

'Gill, you're just not earning your wages!'

'Oh, why not?'

The attendance of these Davidson boys is appalling! What are you going to do about it? Billy will never get his 'O' Grades at this rate!'

'I know he's been off a lot. But the boys have had a rough time recently. They've been in temporary foster care in Dalkeith for three weeks. It's been hard for them to get to school from there.'

'And another thing,' chipped in Alex's technical teacher. 'Why are you letting them go on the field trips? They should be kept in school. Truants should be forced to make up the time they've missed.'

I rose to their defence. 'Ally, these are two very deprived boys. Why should we deprive them even further by denying them the excitement of a week away from the ghetto where they live?'

'You guidance staff are so soft! Discipline's what they need, not holiday camps in the Highlands!' he jibed.

I laughed. I knew he was deliberately trying to

provoke me. 'Oh come on! You know fine the quality of work they'll be doing in school camp. They'll be exposed to a completely different environment and learn social skills they could never learn here!'

'Sit them at a desk,' he pronounced, ' with books in front of them! Too many fal-de-rals did none of them any good.'

Our hard line detractors were never short of words, and I just let him have the last one.

We were very lucky to have Jill on the guidance staff: without her counselling skills and gentle persistence we'd probably never have divined the truth in this sensitive case. It seems likely that much child abuse has gone and still does go undetected partly because it is such a taboo subject, and partly because youngsters simply cannot face the massive consequences likely to result if abuse is uncovered.

The first time I ever suspected a child was being molested was early in my career as a housemistress. The elderly and wise school nurse confidentially revealed that one of my 14-year-old girls, whom we'll call Jenny, had been admitted to hospital with suspected acute appendicitis, but to everyone's astonishment she had given birth to a still-born child. Jenny had wept unceasingly but had resolutely refused to provide any information about the conception.

I was astounded. Jenny was a slight immature

undernourished child: she was very withdrawn, scarcely spoke, and displayed no interest in boys whatsoever. Mrs Owens, the nurse, was equally puzzled, and when I tentatively suggested the stepfather might be involved she concurred.

'Yes,' she said, 'it was very odd. Apparently stepdad accompanied her to hospital, excluded the mother and made all the communications with the medics. Jenny's mother seemed astonished, and absolutely unable to account for it all.'

This occurred some weeks before Jenny reached the school leaving age, and we never actually saw her again. Since the poor girl remained silent there were no grounds for a criminal prosecution, and someone got off scot free, but I sometimes wonder what became of Jenny thereafter.

Evidence of abuse is hard to come by and perhaps on occasion we were not persistent enough. One 12-year-old girl, Ella regularly hung around at the end of school crying because she was reluctant to go home. She went so far as to explain to her (male) guidance teacher that she didn't like her mother's boyfriend. Further conversation revealed Ella objected to the way he touched her. We did take the bull by the horns and consulted the social work department, who set up a meeting attended by Ella, her parents, and the guidance teacher in whom she'd confided. Ella's unease was aired but both parents pooh-poohed the suggestion of inappropriate touching, counter-accusing Ella of being attention-seeking. We never did get to the bottom of this but the more I reflect upon it, the more I'm convinced Ella had a genuine problem, and I only hope we nipped it in the bud by bringing things out into the open.

On another occasion I found myself in a very difficult situation. Elaine, the fourth child in a family with a very violent father, exhibited problem behaviour from the moment she enrolled in secondary school. A bright girl, she was insolent, disobedient and disruptive in every class. No such child can survive for long in an institution, however tolerant, and she soon found a place in our off campus unit which catered for individuals who needed special care. The staff dealing with her suspected such highly disturbed behaviour might result from abuse at home, and suggested I should give her the opportunity to disclose her problem. What an impossible situation for both of us!

I did chat with her, gently suggesting her behaviour must stem from difficulties outside school and I mentioned that sometimes boys and girls erupted in school as a response to being molested, or touched in private places by people who should not be doing this. However she denied there was any such problem and we had to let it go. She did eventually find a place in an excellent boarding school which provided in depth care and counselling for disturbed youngsters and Elaine was completely transformed. In confidence, after Elaine had been in residential school for a considerable period, the staff confirmed our suspicions of abuse and they ultimately gave her assistance to live independently of her parents once she left school.

Chapter 6

Marked by Life for Life

It was Monday morning. The receptionist called me. 'Miss Smith, there's a Mrs. Robertson here waiting to enrol her daughter.'

'Fine,' I said, 'I'll just come along and get them.' It was my job to enrol new students and I hoped this would not be yet another who had blotted her copybook in a different school and was looking for a new start, or worse still, someone recently released from residential care. As it happened, the Robertsons fell into neither category, but they were bad news. They were new to the area, having moved from Northfield, which was generally considered a cut above Muirhouse. The family was downwardly socially mobile.

Mrs. Robertson was well spoken and her slightly refined English accent was curiously at variance with her shabby, down at heel appearance. She was clearly not our run of the mill parent. Seeming ill at ease, she remained standing and I sensed a withdrawnness which did not match her articulacy. I introduced myself and offered her a chair, but she declined the seat.

'I'm afraid I'm in a bit of a hurry. I'm due at work shortly. We've been living in Northfield,' she explained, 'and we've just moved into this area. Jan's in Third Year.'

Jan was somewhat gaunt, and tall like her mother. I turned to her.

'Well, Jan, I'm sure you'd like a seat?'

She sat down and retreated as far back as she could, carefully avoiding my eye.

'Which subjects are you doing, Jan?'

''O' Grade English, Maths, History, Accounting, French, and Biology,' Jan replied, head down and almost muttering.

I was pleased to be admitting a bright girl, for a change. 'Good,' I said. 'We might have some problems fitting you into our timetable, but we'll do our best.'

Mrs. Robertson volunteered, 'Jan's missed a bit of school because of the move....and some other things...' She tailed off.

My heart sank a little. We already had more than our share of problem kids and truants. Mrs. Robertson thought Jan hadn't been at school for four weeks, maybe a little more. The girl was poorly dressed and lacking in confidence. She obviously wanted to keep me at arm's length, and it seemed inappropriate to increase her anxiety by being too inquisitive.

'Okay. I'll get her records from Northfield soon, so don't worry, Mrs Robertson. Now maybe I'd better let you get off to work while I settle Jan in.'

Clearly glad to be making her escape, she left with alacrity, scuffing her way along the corridor at a surprising speed. Since I was due to attend a senior staff meeting within ten minutes, I had time only to concoct Jan's timetable for that day and allocate her to a tutor group. After giving her a note for all her teachers explaining who she was I hurriedly introduced her to her tutor and arranged to see her first thing next day. I then shot off to the meeting, late.

On that same afternoon I was able to make contact with Janine, her recent guidance teacher whom I knew quite well, and was dismayed to find she had only been at her previous school for a year during which time her attendance had been appalling. Janine was relieved to be shifting this burden on to me as they had been about to refer her to their Attendance Committee. The family's move into our area would spare her a lot of work. She told me they hadn't fathomed what Jan's problems were, though she surely had plenty, and she confirmed that she was an able student. Next morning, to my relief and somewhat to my surprise, Jan appeared at my office, albeit thirty minutes late. She had not made it to registration and was very hang-dog.

'Not a very good start,' I said, 'but never mind, you're here and that's good.' I was determined to be positive. 'I've sorted out your timetable as well as I could. How did you manage yesterday?'

'Fine. But I'm a bit behind in most subjects.' She seemed dejected.

'Well you did miss a lot at your last school,' I pointed out, 'but you are an intelligent girl and should be able to catch up if you put your mind to it.'

She was obviously unused to compliments and

went quite pink. 'I'll try to,' she said, and I thought she meant it.

'Was there a reason for your poor attendance in Northfield?' I prodded.

She was hesitant, reflecting the same reticence as her mother. 'We had a lot of family problems,' she said, heavily.

'Ah, yes,' I said rather inadequately. 'Well, if you have problems or anything you want to discuss, it sometimes helps to talk things over. You can talk to me any time and be sure whatever you say will be kept confidential.'

'Right,' she said. 'Thanks, Miss.'

I escorted her to PE and explained to her teacher she'd have to sit out as she had not known to bring her kit – and that was the last we saw of her for a fortnight. I had no complaints from her teachers about her absence because most of them were unaware of her existence, but her tutor kept me informed.

My first action, as they had no phone, was to send the welfare assistant to her home with a note for Mrs. Robertson. She reported back there had been no reply though she felt the curtains were twitching. In view of Jan's poor attendance record I decided to phone the mother at her work in Crawford's bakery, but she was off sick and unavailable so my only alternative was to call on the services of Ian, the

Attendance Officer. When, on his second visit, he found Mrs. Robertson at home, she professed shock that Jan was truanting and denied knowledge of her whereabouts. When Ian had suggested speaking to Jan's father, Mrs. Robertson had become highly alarmed and promised she'd deal with the problem herself.

'You know,' said Ian, 'I wouldn't be surprised if she were a battered wife. She's definitely scared of him.'

The same thought had already occurred to me and when Mrs Robertson again brought Jan in on the Monday my suspicions were strengthened. Her hair was no longer scraped back into its usual bun but was now released, and her long stringy hair was ineffectively concealing a black bruise on the side of her face. Her daughter was positively lugubrious and nursing a bandaged wrist.

'Maybe if you have a chat with Jan that would help,' her mother suggested, before she scuffed off. Was I right in thinking she was limping?

I turned to Jan. 'Well, let's get you sorted.'

She made no response.

'Jan, what is wrong about school?'

'Nothing, really,' she muttered.

'Where do you go when you're off?'

'If my mother's working I stay at home.'

'And otherwise?'

'I go to my married sister's and help her with her bairn.'

'It is the law, Jan. You must attend school. If you don't, you can go to a Children's Panel and could be sent to residential school.'

'I know. I was at a Panel for not attending after my brother –' she stopped and flushed dark red.

'Your brother what?' I asked.

'Did Northfield not tell you?'

'No, you weren't there long. And school records don't usually provide family histories.'

She was silent for what seemed a long time. 'Before we went to Northfield we lived in Liberton. My granny lived two doors away. 'Someone murdered her and stole her savings and – ' she gulped ' – my brother got the blame.'

I said nothing, impassively waiting for further revelations.

'It wasn't him,' she protested, 'but he got a life sentence. He's in Barlinnie now.'

'Is that why you stopped going to school?' I asked her.

'Well, maybe. But there's other reasons too...' There was another long pause as she thought her own dark thoughts.

'Such as?' I finally prompted.

'I worry about my mother.'

'Why is that?'

'Well, it's my father. I hate him! He's a brute!' she said vehemently.

'Does he hit her?'

'Did you see that bruise on her face? He did that! And the reason she was limping was he whacked her on the leg last night because his trousers weren't washed!'

'Does he hit you?'

'Not since I threatened to report him to a social worker. But he's a beast and I wish he was dead!' She was unconsciously wringing her hands, and shaking.

'Is he worse when he's drinking?'

'He's worst when he brings round his friends from the tannery.'

'Women friends?'

'No. Men.' Almost as an aside she added, 'He's a pervert. He takes them into the bedroom and...' she tailed off.

'And what?' I asked quietly, sensing she wanted me to know more.

She finally got it out.... 'He has sex with them.'

'And what does your mother say to this?'

'Nothing! She's petrified of him. She just lets him do what he likes.' She was sobbing now, with her head in her hands.

I handed her a tissue and sat silent for a while. Poor girl. She was a wounded animal, deeply scarred by events in her life, and seeking a refuge to which she could retreat and lick her wounds. I gave some consideration to what she had told me, and wondered what was the best thing to do. It was quite likely she had been subjected to abuse, but I felt she seemed to have taken some control of the situation at home as far as she was concerned, and I decided her revelations of this morning were more than enough for the time being. I spoke quietly.

'Well Jan, I realise you are up against it and I don't want to make life harder for you than it is. I can see why it's hard for you to go to classes, but school is compulsory, so I'll tell you what I can do. I can get you a desk in the corner of my office, and you can come here every day and work here till you get used to us. I can make sure you get assignments for each subject, to work through, and there may be some classes you would feel OK about attending. How about that?'

I knew this arrangement would complicate my life considerably, as I frequently needed privacy for interviews and phone calls, and I would often be away at meetings or taking classes, but this was an extreme case demanding extreme measures. Education was the least of her problems right now.

She raised her head. 'I could give it a try,' she offered.

So that is what we did. She had her own little corner in my office where she sat endlessly writing or reading. If she ran out of work, or couldn't complete her assignments, she read school library books. Our long-suffering staff who were, in the main, sympathetic to youngsters with problems and way out solutions, accepted the situation with little comment, although I was unable to divulge Jan's problems.

Happily, she felt accepted in the Business Studies department and did attend her classes there, and I got on with my job as best I could. When I was out she was able to answer the phone and take messages, and if people came urgently seeking me she usually knew where I could be found. Her attendance was by no means perfect, but we limped along, her life still punctuated by various crises initiated by her father.

She kept me up to date with news of her brother Fergus whom she and her mother occasionally visited in Barlinnie, and she always stuck up for him. Things being what they were, she had no friends, but she did see her sister quite often and was devoted to her little nephew. She did tell me her sister and Fergus had been subjected to abuse by their father but that she hadn't because they had protected her from him. It was clear from the work she did in her corner that she had a lot of academic potential, sadly never realised in school. Her self esteem was non-existent, but I did emphasise to her that she was bright and had ability and, though she had nothing to show from school, she could easily gain Highers if she was ever of a mind to go to college after she left.

Her leaving, if it could be called that, was gradual, in that in her last term of compulsory education her attendance deteriorated to the point where she was off for the last four weeks. There was nothing to be done to improve things at this stage, if indeed, I was minded to try. The wheels of officialdom would never catch up with her in the timescale available.

I did not see Jan for about another ten years, by when we had become a fully fledged community school. I was surprised to meet her in the foyer one day; she was with a tall unshaven fellow and had a small boy clutching her hand. I greeted her with pleasure, glad to see she was still around. She in turn introduced me to her partner, George, and their son Rory. She had worked as a cleaner but the couple were now studying Higher English together and seeking qualifications in order to find better paid work. I was so pleased to realise she was making a life for herself and had found a partner whose intellect seemed to match hers.

When, some years later, I read in the newspaper that her brother Fergus had been released from prison and then been arrested quite soon thereafter for another very violent offence, I fervently hoped she had developed enough stability and resilience to be able to cope with yet another of life's blows. I think, as a child, she knew in her heart that Fergus had been responsible for her grandmother's death, but refused to admit it, even to herself. In fact, the whole family was probably using denial as a way of coping with the horrendous slur which would stick to them if they admitted to having a murderer in the family.

Chapter 7

Arran Idyll

The school was buzzing. It was April and, while all the senior students were preparing for exams, the second and third years were going on their annual field trips. As usual, I was taking a motley collection of girls to Whiting Bay in Arran. They were few in number but if their normal behaviour was anything go by the week was likely to be quite challenging. However, along with my co-leaders Mae and Janet, I was looking forward to a change of scene, and hoping for the best.

The pre-camp meeting was our first test and it took some time before the girls calmed down. 'This is the programme,' I announced, holding up a huge timetable. 'As you can see, we're not going for a holiday, but it will be fun.'

'Dae we get any free time, Miss?' asked Wilma whose main interest in life was boys.

'Not a lot, but enough. You don't want to get bored.'

'Ah hope there's a telly,' was Mandy's contribution.

'Well there is one in the Youth Hostel, but we do have to share it,' said Mae.

'Oh, we'll no get tae see "Corrie", ' complained Donna.

'You'll probably be too busy doing other things,' consoled Mae.

Our aim was too keep them so busy they had no time to make trouble. This of course took its toll on the staff who would be on duty round the clock, and investing vast amounts of energy on persuading the girls to expend vast amounts of energy. Though it was just a drop in the ocean, we'd decided each leader would have one precious morning or afternoon to chill out.

'Hey!' shouted Carol Anne, 'There's a barbecue on Thursday night!'

'Brill!' exclaimed Jessie.

'Right,' I interrupted, 'let's go through the

programme from the start.'

The girls were wildly excited at the prospect of getting away, but we wanted them to be clear they were going on an educational trip, and to divest them of any false expectations of living in palatial accommodation and following an undemanding do-as-you-please programme. As well as mentioning attractions like pony-trekking and swimming, we majored on the ethic of doing daily chores in the hostel and the need to take turns of cooking meals and washing up afterwards. They seemed undaunted, probably because for most of them domestic duties and child-care were the daily norm.

The school would provide sleeping bags, boots, day sacks and cagoules, but the pupils had to bring the personal basic necessities we had listed. Even then, we knew from experience there would be those who had no nightwear, or items like towels which their household could not do without for the week. Several kids would turn up with only a few skimpy possessions in a supermarket carrier bag, but would survive the week, and even thrive, in spite of that.

One Monday a week later the fateful day arrived. Our group, having a ferry to catch, assembled early: mountains of equipment had to be packed into the minibus, and food and packed lunches collected from the kitchen. Mae was in charge of the food and also took responsibility for seeing that all workbooks, stationery, first aid, maps, menus, reference books et al were safely stowed away under the seats. Several parents had come for the send off, many bringing baby-filled buggies and dogs, so the scene was fairly chaotic as we tried to calm the loud-mouthed pupils and shoehorn them into the van. I was nervous we might miss the ferry – it was eighty-four miles to Ardrossan and we had to embark at eleven thirty. I felt mightily relieved when everything was finally ready and we trundled out of the playground with the barking of dogs and screamed farewells ringing in our ears.

Janet had distributed clipboards, pencils and a worksheet to everyone, so after they had all opened their many bags of sweets the first few miles were taken up with trying to follow the map and filling in answers to questions about the journey, to the accompaniment of appreciative sucking noises. We had only reached West Calder before the peace was broken.

'Miss, will we be having a toilet stop?'

'Oh Tracy, did you not go before we left? We're rushing to get to the ferry and haven't much time .'

'Ah did go but Ah'm always like this when Ah'm excited.'

'We're in the middle of the countryside,' I

exclaimed. 'There's no toilets here. Can you go behind a bush?'

This suggestion was met with horror from Tracy and incredulous laughter from the rest.

'Well, we'll stop in half an hour. Can you wait that long?'

'Aye, Ah'll just have tae cross my legs,' was the answer.

As a distraction Mae referred them to their worksheets, and began pointing out the farm animals in the fields we were passing.

'Can anyone see a sheep with twin lambs? What do you call a female sheep?'

She was encouraged by the answers and as we passed fields of cattle she began imparting information. 'See these black cows with white bands round their middles? They're Belted Galloways. Farmers call them 'belties' because of their white belts.'

She moved on to some difficult questions. 'Anyone know the difference between beef cows and milk cows?'

With no hesitation Teresa replied, 'Beef cows are brown'.

Janet, beside me and choking with mirth, muttered, 'There's an udder answer to that!'

And amazingly, no one else seemed to know any

better! Somehow, to the accompaniment of her colleagues' giggles, Mae braved her way through that one and moved on to something quite different.

'What's this place called? Yes, Darvel. And what famous person was born here?'

No answer.

'How are we supposed to know that?' queried Ellen.

'Keep looking. Right, see that sign?'

I slowed down so they wouldn't miss it.

'Aye.' Teresa redeemed herself. 'It says "Birthplace of Alexander Fleming"'.

'Well done. What did he discover?'

Blank faces.

'Telephones?' suggested Wilma.

'Naw,' said Jessie. 'It was penicillin. It was in wee print on that sign.'

'Well spotted, Jessie,' said Mae, sinking back into her seat before muttering, ' Your turn to amuse them, Janet. I'm exhausted.'

Luckily, because Tracy was agitating again, we were almost at Loudon where we could stop for the toilet. I pulled into the supermarket car park.

'You have exactly 15 minutes', I announced. 'Come back in time or we'll miss the boat. Make sure you take out all you need. I'm locking the van.'

They made for the entrance and disappeared

into the toilets while we three leaders went in the direction of a quick cuppa in the cafe.

On emerging we found that, true to type, Wilma and Shona were back at the van, chatting up three teenage boys while the rest of our gang straggled back loaded with yet more crisps and sweets. With difficulty we managed to get everyone in, the boy daft ones embarking last with many a backward glance. As we pulled out of the car park Shona and Wilma waved enthusiastically to the three lads, their faces pressed to the window.

'I don't know why you're bothering,' said Janet. 'You're never going to see them again!'

'Aye, Ah ken,' said Wilma. 'Makes ye want tae greet, doesn't it?'

However they sat back quite cheerfully with no sign of tears and, while their friends grazed relentlessly on their new supplies, the two spent the next bit of the journey trying to decide which boy they liked most.

Soon they had the distraction of viewing the island of Arran and were easily persuaded to answer the last two questions on their worksheets before tidying their clipboards away for a spell.

When we reached the pier the minibus joined the queue of cars waiting in line for the ferry, which was still out at sea, and in the short time before embarking everyone took the chance to explore the waiting room, buy more supplies from the slot machines, and – guess what – pay yet another visit to the toilets.

As we wanted the girls to enjoy boarding the boat, Mae and Janet gave them their tickets and, when the time came, led them up the gangway while I manoeuvred and parked the van on the car deck before rejoining the group for a quiet briefing in the lounge. We set the troops loose after some reminders about keeping safe and, using their terms, 'not giving us a red face' by their behaviour.

They spent the next hour noisily exploring the ship and feeding the remains of their sandwiches to the gulls while the staff, pretending not to know them, made efforts to recruit their strength with greasy pies and strong coffee in the cafeteria.

Finally, we all clambered down to the car deck and squeezed back into the van before trundling off the ferry behind a coach and several lorries. As the hostel was not open till four o'clock we were in no hurry and decided to drive through Brodick for some fun playing crazy golf before lumbering off to Whiting Bay. Fortunately we had the course to ourselves. I doubt whether any of the girls had ever held a putter before, let alone attempted to use one, and consequently the 'golf' was even crazier than the attendant was used to. On the concrete surface even timidly hit balls travelled great distances and, to the accompaniment of shrieks and groans, several first balls aiming at cup number one reached holes eight or nine, and one even went as far as the road! Some girls enjoyed the challenge and the opportunity to play the fool, while others, struggling incompetently to direct the balls through tiny tunnels and over narrow bridges, found the novelty palled quite quickly.

After twenty minutes the less gifted accepted the offer to go trampolining and Mae walked them across to the beach park. There, even the least agile seemed to perform well enough to enjoy themselves but once the 'golfers' arrived they were quite happy to relinquish their places to them and become spectators.

By three o'clock it was time to be on our way, but not without a trip to the execrable public lavatories. The staff, seeing the graffitti scored walls and the floors awash with water, decided to forego this oppportunity, but the less fastidious pupils surged in without qualms, though Tracy's comment on exit was worth recording.

'Gawd, ye dinnae ken if ye're in here for a piddle or a paddle!' she exclaimed as she sloshed out through the puddles.

We set out for our destination only eight miles away, and as they focused their attention on the scenery, our urban townies revealed their reactions.

'Is that a' the shops?' asked Carol Anne. 'Whit does everybody dae here? The scenery's nice but whae would want tae live here?'

'No me. Ah didnae see a cinema, did you?' replied another.

'What'll we do in our free time?' asked the normally withdrawn Ellen. ' There's only trees and bushes here!'

'Good job we'll no have much free time!' replied Jessie, a sentiment silently echoed by the staff.

Just before we reached the hostel, I pulled in and parked at the side of the road. With some effort I managed to silence the group in order to deliver some stern words. 'We're almost at the hostel', I told them, 'so I want you to pay attention to what I say now.'

I broke off to glare at Margie who was creating a diversion by blowing a huge bubble of gum through her teeth.

'Sorry,' she muttered, as she hastily sucked it back in.

'We're sharing this hostel with other people and we must be careful and considerate towards them,' I lectured.

'And remember the rules about bedtimes and

keeping quiet. You've got them in writing. I don't want one single complaint from the warden about your behaviour. Anyone who steps out of line will be punished. I have taken badly behaved pupils home before – but surely it won't come to that with you! Anyone want to ask anything before we go on in?'

'Miss, dae the teachers sleep in our rooms with us?' asked Tracy.

'No-o-o, we have a separate room.' I'd fought hard with the warden for this privilege and won, on condition that the girls behaved. 'But we will come and sleep with you if you misbehave!' I threatened.

'Aye, she will,' confirmed Shona, sotto voce. 'She slept in my sister's dorm last year!'

I was quite pleased my reputation had gone before. It was a help.

'Anything else? No.............? OK. Let's go.'

And so we arrived.

Tuesday

Everyone appeared at 8.15am for breakfast, though most were bleary-eyed and some were more dishevelled than others. Clearly they hadn't slept soundly, though having been well warned they had all, except for one, been quiet enough to escape my wrath. Poor Tracy, the first to break the silence after

11pm, had been unceremoniously dragged from bed at her first sound and forced to bring her mattress through to sleep on the floor of the teachers' room. All was now forgiven however, and her friends felt free to make fun of her over breakfast

'Aye. That's the longest sleep Ah've had since Ah wis a bairn!' Tracy lied.

Each of us was responsible for her own breakfast; for most it was meagre and for some it was nothing but a glass of juice. I was glad no one was making my meal: last year on returning home I'd made the horrifying discovery that I had threadworms. Only Mae, the quartermaster, was privy to this because I wanted her to be very sure the girls on kitchen duty thoroughly washed their hands.

We each prepared a packed lunch because we would be out from 10.30am till at least 4.30pm. The girls were amazed and amused to see a Welsh boy struggling to make custard for breakfast and audibly wishing he'd brought his mother with him, and Donna and Tracy had their fun.

'So that's what the Welsh live on', giggled Donna, but she kindly helped him make it without lumps.

The day was dull and the forecast poor but we had plenty of waterproofs so undaunted, all of us having done our allotted chores, we lumbered out with our daysacks and clipboards to board the van.

Once we reached the hilltop between Lamlash and Brodick, we parked the van and prepared to walk over the ridge and down to the shore at Clauchlands. Several had donned wellies, but when Janet proffered the conspicuous red cagoules she was firmly rebuffed.

'Ah'm no wearin' that,' protested Tracy.

'Me neither,' agreed Shona. 'Makes ye look a tramp!'

It wasn't raining but it soon would be. Janet persevered. 'You're going to get wet.'

'Naw, we'll be fine,' was the defiant consensus, so she didn't force the issue.

Twenty minutes later, as we struggled up the overgrown woodland path, the heavens opened, fulfilling Janet's prophecy. Give the girls their due, they made no complaint as the rain poured down relentlessly, wetting them through in minutes. One little drama focused their attention elsewhere for a brief time. Seeing a movement in the heather, Carol Anne bent down for a closer look.

'Snake! A snake!' she yelled in terror.

Everyone laughed thinking she was fooling around, but no, she was quite right. I caught sight of an adder slithering through the long grass with its unmistakeable v-pattern on its head. When I confirmed this the stragglers suddenly speeded up and lagged behind no longer, perhaps thinking there would be safety in numbers.

The mist obligingly lifted and the rain stopped as we reached the top of the ridge and we could enjoy the magnificent view of the Sleeping Warrior above Brodick Bay to the left, and the Holy Isle and Lamlash to the right. We picnicked in the shelter of some rocks though the dampness and a keen wind did not encourage us to linger. Janet turned back downhill to drive the minibus back to meet us at the Point, while the rest of us began picking our way down towards the shore. When our route led us through a herd of cows our city girls were ill at ease. The cows, as cows do, gazed at us with interest. When one took a step in our direction and another made to follow, Tracy could contain herself no longer.

'Run! They're chasin' us!' she yelled, suiting her actions to her words.

We knew we would be chased if we ran so with some difficulty we managed to deter the others from following suit. Meantime Tracy, well ahead, catapulted herself through the nearest fence into the next field, which was luckily cowless. We couldn't understand why she was calling for help till we caught up on her and peered over the gorse hiding her from view. Having recklessly leapt into a morass of glutinous mud she was stuck in it, and still sinking! Luckily she was wearing wellies and Mae and I managed to haul her out without joining her. A loud laugh went up from the assembled onlookers when they realised Tracy had been rescued, but not her wellies, which were still stuck there. Mae, brave soul, removed her boots and rolled up her jeans; as she fished out the wellies with the aid of a stick the girls cheered.

'Good for you!' exclaimed Shona. 'Ah wouldnae dae that for a' the tea in China!'

Our little crisis over, we straggled down to the seashore path, in good spirits but somewhat the worse for wear. The weather was better but the girls were covered in mud and soaked through. Realising they could scarcely be wetter, they began pushing each other into deep puddles and madly splashing us all as we passed. It was funny.

'What would the Heidie say if he saw us now?' yelled Wilma, echoing my own thoughts.

Soon we reached the rendezvous with Janet but it was clear we were in no state to do the land use survey we'd planned – our priority was to get the girls dry and have a change of clothes. We ditched the planned programme and made for the hostel. Though it was still closed we persuaded the warden to let us in for twenty minutes to towel ourselves dry and put on other clothing, after which we piled back into the van and proceeded to Kildonan beach for an impromptu seal count and a shell competition.

When we finally got back the evening passed quickly. Cooking, dining and doing chores took up time, after which the girls wrote up their log books and spent a good hour preparing a quiz and making sweets to take when we visited the old people's home the next evening.

Wednesday

More rain and mist. Not unexpectedly, the girls donned their red cagoules without a murmur even before they entered the van. We were off to Blackwaterfoot to ponytrek and everyone was up to high doh. Luckily we had left plenty of time for the journey, because we had only travelled a few miles before our next adventure befell. Mae asked me to slow down and pointed out several orphan lambs being fed close to the road. This was too good a chance to miss so I parked the van and Mae went to ask if we could come and help. The farmer's wife was delighted to have a little respite and the girls were entranced by the tiny lambs. None had fed a lamb before but most had had experience of human babies; with cries of delight they deftly picked up their lambs and applied the bottles. It was impossible to tell whether the girls or the lambs derived more pleasure from the process. A poor spring for lambing had resulted in eight lambs having to be fed several times a day – a chore for the farm staff but an unforgettable experience for our girls. Every girl posed for a picture feeding her lamb and, later on, proudly displayed it to anyone who showed the slightest interest.

With difficulty we tore ourselves away and resumed our journey to the stables.

'Has anyone ever been on a pony?' asked Janet, and received varied replies.

'Hundreds of times!' answered Linda. 'I help at Silverknowes on Saturdays.'

'Ah'm terrified o' horses,' confided Ellen.

'Ah've been on the donkeys at Blackpool –' said Jessie.

'–But that's no the same as pony-riding!' interrupted Teresa.

Linda felt confident enough to offer plenty of advice. 'Dinnae stand behind a horse – it might kick ye!' and 'If ye make a sudden noise ye might get thrown off!' and frighteningly, 'If yer pony starts tae roll jump off or it'll roll over you!'

Mae, afraid of the effect Linda was having on the more timid ones, broke in. 'Oh look! That's the stables! We're nearly there.'

In five minutes we were on the lane leading to the stables; the excited chatter died to a murmur as nervousness took over. Even Linda lost her bravado.

'Ah'm gonnae ask for a quiet yin,' muttered Shona.

'Could Ah get that wee yin?' asked Ellen, pointing to the most diminutive.

'You might be too tall for a wee one,' said Mae, 'but don't worry – the stable girls'll sort you out.'

As soon as we disembarked we were each given a hard hat, and led into the tack room where we were allocated ponies according to our size and experience. We then finally met our respective ponies standing patiently in the yard.

Ellen was happy to be given the smallest, little Star, and Mae and I, who had had some experience, mounted huge ex-police horses, David and Goliath! The girls couldn't start soon enough and, after minimal basic instruction, we set off in line, making our way across the field towards the shore.

As we rode through long grass, ignoring the drizzle, disaster suddenly struck. There was a sudden loud gunshot and every pony bolted! After a moment spent controlling my startled Goliath I looked around and was appalled to see, hunched in the long wet grass, at least eight unmoving red-clad bundles with their ponies close by. Already envisaging lurid newspaper headlines, I joined the stable girls in riding over to help. What a relief to see the red bundles struggle to their feet apparently uninjured! Mae and Janet were also intact. The lead rider loudly cursed whoever had activated a bird scarer without warning the stable, as her helpers checked the girls and then encouraged them to remount.

The proud Linda suffered the ignominy of being boosted back up into the saddle, but said nothing.

'Ah telt ye Ah'd fall off,' said Ellen.

'Ye're no the only one,' grumbled Teresa, rubbing a sore arm as she remounted. 'Ah'm soaked!'

The girls were tough and continued without a murmur, though perhaps with a little less confidence. The rather tame trek alongside the golf course was an accomplishment for them and, when they finally dismounted after an hour, stiff and smelly, they had a sense of achievement and plenty of stories to tell.

The rest of the afternoon was taken up picnicking, beachcombing and swimming in the hotel pool.

'We'll all smell clean for the oldies tonight,' rejoiced Mae, sotto voce.

Later, Shona and Mandy produced pie, beans and chips for dinner, followed by ice cream and tinned pears and then everyone gathered for another pep talk before we descended on 'Cooriedoon', the home for the elderly. I rehearsed the programme.

'We'll be there for an hour and a half,' I announced. 'The first half hour we'll just move round the residents in pairs, chatting to them –'

'Ah'm no used tae old folk,' burst out Jessie. 'What'll we say to them?'

'Good question – any suggestions?'

'Ah just talk tae ma grannie aboot when she was young,' said Linda.

'Aye, and I think they'd like tae speak aboot their grandchildren,' suggested Tracy.

'Two good ideas,' I said. 'I'm sure you'll manage fine. After a blether we'll do the team quiz you've all prepared and then we'll have supper in the dining room.'

'When dae we gi'e them the sweeties we made?' asked Jessie.

After discussion we agreed to hand them out in the first part of the evening – they would help the conversation.

My secret misgivings about landing the girls on the old people were happily unfounded. I was pleasantly surprised by their understanding of the old ladies' limitations, and by their ease as they chattered to them and engaged their interest. I realised most of them had grannies for whom they were expected to accept some responsibility.

The evening was a great success, and both staff

and residents expressed their appreciation of all the girls' efforts. The girls' self esteem rose measurably –they were much more used to blame than praise– and they were in high spirits as we made our way homewards. Predictably, it all went to their heads: it was no easy matter to calm them down by 11pm, and, in fact, Mae ended up taking herself and her sleeping bag into the spare bed in the dorm where two girls simply refused to settle. All of them hated it, but they all had a much needed eight hours of sleep, and I was able to evade a nasty confrontation with the warden.

Thursday

We had an appointment at Lamlash High School for 10.30am, to let our pupils meet local girls in the hope that both groups might catch glimpses of life in communities very different from their own. Mae's questionnaire, engineered to widen the exchange from the limits of the teen culture, proved useful, and after their initial shyness, they were all soon chattering.

One question, about getting up in the morning, generated a lot of interest.

'You get up at 5.30!' exclaimed the astonished

Shona. 'What on earth for?'

'School's an hour and a half away, and I have to feed the hens and collect eggs before I go,' was the answer.

'Well,' said Tracy, 'I thought I was bad! I'm supposed to leave at 7 to do my paper round and be at school for 8.30!'

Janet's eyebrows rose. 'Now we know why she's never in time!' she muttered.

One girl inquired about life out of school in the big city.

'It's pretty boring here. I have an hour to get home in the school bus. Then I have dinner, do my homework and go to bed! Slicing swedes is our big excitement!'

'Well,' said Jessie, 'I take five minutes to walk home, but I usually have to shop for my granny and make the tea for the family before my Ma gets back from work. If Ah've money Ah sometimes get to go to the disco on Saturdays but me and Ellen usually just go to the chippie'.

The grass on the other side was not particularly greener.

Many of the country girls were put off from studying beyond the age of sixteen because it entailed living on the mainland from Monday to Friday, in a school hostel. But Tracy and Mandy could think of nothing nicer than the freedom of being away from home and all the domestic chores expected of them.

Once this exchange was over we were shown round the school before being entertained in the school canteen with Irn Bru and biscuits which the girls fell upon and totally consumed. We ended our visit with regret and gave our hostesses a warm invitation to visit us in Edinburgh.

'Aye', said Mandy, 'you could camp in our school gym and cook meals in the Home Ec. Department!'

'An' ye could swim in the school pool and watch videos in the film room,' suggested another.

'Yes,' chipped in Ellen, 'and we could take you around.'

Their enthusiasm made me realise we could have profited from a longer visit. Maybe next time.

As we parted Mrs. Lough obviously felt the same. 'Maybe one day we'll take up your invitation,' she laughed as we left.

In fact, about eighteen months later she did – but that's another story.

From the High School we made a dash for Glen Rosa, a must for all visitors to Arran. Leaving the van near the campsite, we set off up the glen, our daysacks full of lunch. We aimed to picnic at 'the slidey pool' about two miles up the glen.

With Goatfell towering up on our right we

strode up the track in the sunshine, negotiating in turn potholes and rutted mud. There was a brisk wind and we were lucky to spot several red deer below the higher ridges on both sides of the glen. Unfortunately, as the path deteriorated, some of the initial enthusiasm waned. In order to take the girls' minds off the hardships of thirst, hunger and the demanding terrain which were taking their toll we had to resort to ridiculous fantasies.

'It's OK,' said Janet. 'There's an ice cream van just round that corner!'

'Aye!' was Margie's sarcastic reply, 'and ten-pin bowling and a disco club!'

'Ah cannae wait tae get tae the luxury swimming pool,' dreamed Linda.

'An' slide down the flumes,' chimed in Teresa.

We needed our stories to keep us going. The last half mile was along narrow boulder-strewn sheep paths which kept petering out in bogs and we were hungry and unkempt when we arrived at the pool.

The scene, however, was enchanting. On either side of our flattish valley were steep, rocky, heather-clad slopes, and ahead of us was a jagged alpine ridge, part of the 'Sleeping Warrior', silhouetted against blue sky.

The girls subsided into the heather beside the stream and fell upon their sandwiches. Clear water rolled over a small waterfall before gathering in a deep black pool and spilling out shallowly over some rocks lower down.

'Miss,' said Mary Kennoway, 'can we swim in the pool?'

It was very inviting. I had splashed in it many times in summer, and although this was only May, I was sorely tempted. Janet was aware of this.

'I'll go in if you do!' she challenged me, and in a moment of madness we began stripping to our underwear.

Mary, looking on this as assent, beat us to it and was soon standing poised on a flat rock, modelling her charming black and orange bra and pants. I had removed my jeans and boots before I got cold feet, in both senses. Janet, having removed her boots and anorak, felt the biting wind and hastily changed her tune.

'I think not,' was her verdict.

After a few minutes of goading from the girls and dipping our toes in the icy water, our courage failed us.

'Oh Miss, ye've let me down!' Mary feigned disappointment, but I sensed she was relieved not to experience her baptism of ice. We hastily resumed our clothes after many jibes and set off on the return walk.

The picture of Mary in her orange polka-dotted underwear was indelibly engraved on my memory and every time after this, when in more sober moments we passed in the school corridors, our eyes met and smiles hovered on our lips as we mutually recalled the scene.

Those with cash left did some last minute shopping in Brodick on the way back, and we finally reached the hostel with some time left for packing and cleaning before our evening activity, a beach barbecue at King's Cross Point. At our five o'clock meal which consisted of a scrappy and unbalanced collection of soup, pasta, tuna, biscuits, crisps and custard, we consumed all our leftovers, and by seven, after our packing was completed, we could leave for the beach. Mae walked there with three miscreants being punished for having been caught earlier smoking behind the rocks in Glen Rosa, while the more virtuous were taken by minibus.

On arrival we set to, gathering driftwood and choosing stones to encircle the fire. Bonfires were a novelty to the group and it was hard to motivate them to collect the huge amount of fuel we needed, but fortunately Mae and her crew arrived shortly, staggering under great bundles of wood in an attempt to redeem themselves.

'Will this put us in your good books now?' joked

Donna.

'Oh no, this is worth a real reward,' protested Wilma. 'I demand A passes in the exams for this! Look at my fleece! It's covered in moss and mud.'

'That'll come off!' moaned Shona. 'When will I get rid of this?' she asked, pointing to a scratch on her chin.

'If you don't stop greetin' the tide'll come in before the fire's lit!' answered Mae. 'Come on!'

'Oh please Miss, can Ah light the fire?' pleaded Margie.

Lighting open fires was a new experience for most of the girls, whose homes were mostly gas fuelled.

'Oh curses, Ah wanted tae dae that,' said Shona.

'No need to swear. You can both have a go, one on either side.'

There was a race for the matchbox.

'This match won't light,' complained Margie, scrubbing it against the sandpaper.

'Well you've had plenty practice at lighting matches!' laughed Carol, pretending to puff at a cigarette.

'Mine will!' triumphed Shona as she put a light to the kindling and stood back to watch a flame shoot up.

Margie set her side on fire at the third attempt and watched fascinated as it caught fire.

After the initial pleasure in seeing the fire take hold, they waited with mounting impatience for the bonfire to blaze and mature to a point where they could sizzle their sausages. Meanwhile Janet explained the cooking method which involved impaling sausages on sticks and holding them over red hot embers. When we finally got going some tragedies struck.

'Oh! Ma sausage's fallen off!' yelled Tracy, who was soon given a replacement.

Linda was less lucky. 'Ow! Dinnae drip that sausage on ma jeans!' she wailed at someone. 'Ma leg's burnin'!'

The hot fat burn on her leg was given first aid by Mae, who soothed her skin, and her feelings, with remarkable skill.

Everyone else was reasonably successful, though some who'd refused to listen to Janet's plea for patience ended up with sausages burnt black on the outside and almost raw in the middle. Others accidentally set their cooking sticks on fire and had to be rescued. However, before long, everyone had a reasonably edible sausage inside her roll and was able to sit down to eat and drink.

'We can dae this in the back green when the gas meter runs oot!' joked Teresa.

'Aye', responded Ellen, 'and Ah'll phone the Fire

Brigade!'

Suddenly Janet surprised us by producing black, roasted potatoes, after poking around in the ashes. We all sampled them but they were very burnt on the outside as well as being extremely hot, so it was hard to access the edible parts and most of us gave up . However it was a universally popular move when Mae distributed marshmallows for toasting. More sizzling meant adding more layers of dirt to our already sooty hands and faces, and we reeked of smoke, but who cared?

'If ma mother could see me now!' laughed Jessie.

'Or even smell you...' added Teresa.

The girls' fascination with fire meant we had no problems getting them to gather all scraps and rubbish lying around: they took great pleasure in throwing it on to the fire and watching it blaze. Even extinguishing the fire was fun as we drenched it with sea water and then covered the embers with sand and stones. A raucous beach concert followed, with the girls doing impromptu turns. In one challenging act individuals were invited to test their mettle by demonstrating how long they could stand in a small circle and have buckets of sea water thrown at them with great force. I was thankful they'd be taking their wet dirty clothes home to be washed! Everyone ended up soaked, so much so that only

Teresa and Mae were dry enough to return in the bus and everyone else had to jog back in the dusk along the coastal path with Janet.

Happily the extra exercise defused their remaining energy, making the last night unexpectedly less fraught for the staff: physical exhaustion took over and propelled them to bed far quicker than we could have hoped!

Friday

Aware there was much to be done, we staggered out of bed at 7am and wakened the campers with some difficulty.

'Wakey, wakey!' called Mae, disgustingly cheerful. 'We're going home today!'

'Could we no stay the weekend?' groaned Carol. 'Ah like it here.'

'No fears', said Jessie. 'Ah'm dyin' tae get back tae the telly!'

'Aye,' was Ellen's sarcastic reply, 'and the baby-minding, and shopping for ma gran, and doing all the dishes...'

'Well, you're lucky your Mum's got a job,' said Jessie. 'At least you get pocket money!'

'GET UP!' yelled Mae. 'We've to be at the boat

for 10, and we've packing, breakfast, clearing up and cleaning to do! Jump to it!'

She rarely shouted, so when she did, as now, they knew she meant it, and everyone jumped, or in some cases crawled, to it.

Amazingly, we met our deadline and made our farewells at the hostel with a mixture of relief, on the part of the staff anyway, and regret on the part of most of the girls.

'Oh God, it's raining,' complained Tracy getting out of the van at the pier.

'No need to tell God that,' said Janet. 'He knows – He made the rain!'

Tracy gazed at her blankly, failing to get the point.

As I lined up the van in the queue for the car ferry, everyone spilled out on to the tarmac for a last foray to the shops, with Mae in attendance, before straggling up the pier to board the boat. Slumped over the steering wheel and feeling the adrenaline draining slowly out of me, I congratulated myself on yet another field trip eventfully but successfully accomplished. I could hardly wait for the rest and freedom which would be my reward once I got home.

Chapter 8

Beaten but Unbeaten

Jim invariably sat quietly in a corner of the classroom, only speaking when spoken to. Even then he was monosyllabic, always keeping me at arm's length. Unlike his peers, he never made trouble and was a pleasure to have in class but his sustained withdrawal was unnatural and I worried about him. His younger sister Jackie could not have been more different. From the moment she enrolled in school she stood out, and my attention was soon drawn to her.   Dave, a Modern Studies teacher and keen cyclist, strolled into my office one morning.

'You'll never guess what happened yesterday,' he remarked.

'No. What?' I replied.

'Jackie Wright and Marilyn Macdonald skipped school yesterday afternoon. I met them in Bruntsfield at 4.15.'

'Oh no,' I groaned. 'What happened?'

'Well they saw me cycling over the Links and stopped me because they'd lost their way home.'

'How on earth did they get there?' I gasped.

'After a bit they admitted they'd used their dinner money to get on the bus and they just sat on the top deck touring around all afternoon!'

'But why Bruntsfield?'

Their money had run out and the driver put them off at the Meadows. They hadn't the faintest idea where they were and didn't know how to get home!'

'They must have been very pleased to see you!'

'They were!   I'm their tutor and they were delighted to see a 'kent face'!'

'That's incredible. They're barely twelve years old. Just imagine what could have happened to them...'

'Yes,' said Dave, 'they were quite lucky.'

'Well, thanks for telling me – I'll need to take this further.'

When I finally had a spare half hour I checked the timetable and phoned their French teacher to ask her to send them over, apologising for taking them out of class.

'That pair!' she exclaimed. 'I'll be glad of a respite from them – they are a menace!'

Before long they signalled their arrival with a knock on the door, so I donned my most forbidding glare and bade them come in. Detecting a sense of guilt in their body language I went straight to the point. 'Why did you two skip school yesterday afternoon?'

They glanced briefly at each other before Jackie took on the role of spokesman.

'We had to go and pay Marilyn's mother's electric bill – she was going to be cut off.'

I decided to call their bluff and made to pick up the phone. 'Ah yes. Maybe I'll just call your Mum at her work,' I said to Marilyn. 'What's her number?'

They were both quite discomfited and before Marilyn could formulate a reply Jackie, realising they were defeated, made up her mind to come clean.

'Well, that was really just a story,' she said.

'A lie, you mean – a downright lie!' I feigned anger. 'First of all you truant and then make things worse by telling me some ridiculous story! I want the truth, and the whole truth or I'll just phone your parents and get them up here right now.'

The likelihood of my achieving that was minimal but they irrationally believed I would, and both paled at the thought. I felt slightly guilty as they were probably visualising their parents resorting to violence, but they did need to learn a lesson.

'Oh Miss,' pleaded Jackie, 'dinnae dae that. We'll tell ye what happened...'

Marilyn chipped in. 'Aye. It was just that we hadnae done our maths homework, and we played truant because Mr Jameson is terribly strict.'

'And...?' I questioned.

'We used our dinner money to go up town in the bus.'

'Did you not realise Mr Johnston would tell me he met you?'

'The grass,' muttered Jackie under her breath.

'What?'

'We were on the grass when he cycled past,' explained Marilyn quickly.

'Oh really, well you're on the carpet now,' I retorted, 'and three things are going to happen!'

At this moment we were inconveniently interrupted by the phone and as I answered I heard Jackie mutter despairingly about the belting she'd get at home.

'You're going to repay Mr Johnson the fares he

lent you, and while you're in detention for the next two Wednesday afternoons you're going to make up the maths you missed. I will leave you to explain to your parents what happened when you take home the detention slips for them to sign.'

Visibly relieved that I would not be directly confronting their parents, they agreed to report to me after lunch on the Wednesdays, bringing the Maths work with them. I thought it was unlikely they would breathe a word of their doings to their parents, but hoped the threat of their finding out and giving them a pasting would perhaps keep them in line for a bit.

'You're getting off lightly this time,' I emphasised, 'but if you ever skip school again the Attendance Officer will be at your door immediately! Understand?'

They nodded, and skipped off with alacrity as soon as I dismissed them, leaving me mentally berating myself for being too soft. However I knew I had by no means seen the last of them.

Before long Jonesy, the school cook, reported finding Jackie smoking behind the kitchens, and I knew my forebodings were well founded. It seemed a good idea to consult the head of the primary school Jackie had recently left, so I lifted the phone.

'Jackie Wright!' she exclaimed. 'I'm glad she's

your pigeon now. She was trouble from the word go... though in some ways I couldn't help liking her.'

'Know much about the family?' I asked.

'Not really. The parents didn't frequent the school - we never saw them at Parents' Evenings. Her brother Jim was a completely different kettle of fish. A total nonentity. He just merged in with the wallpaper and nothing we tried could change him.'

'Yes, worryingly withdrawn don't you think?'

'That's true. He could have done with more attention but he was in a class with a dozen or so hell-raisers and he helped to dilute them... If Jim doesn't come out of his shell I think he should see the psychologist.'

'And what are the chances of parental consent for that?'

'Pretty slight, I would say.'

'Yes but it's worth a try, I suppose. And have you any wisdom to impart about Jackie?'

'Oh no. She's a survivor. She'll make it through the jungle whatever you throw at her!'

With these words she left me to plough my own furrow and I decided that her punishment this time would be a reading of the riot act and a letter home.

A month or so later I had the head of Home Economics on the phone.

'Are you free to come over to B1? You're on call and we're having a problem with Jackie Wright.'

Abandoning some paperwork, I swiftly made for B1.

Maggie explained that after being reprimanded for fighting with her cookery partner, Jackie's behaviour had completely disintegrated. Instead of stirring her white sauce she had been flicking someone's legs with a wet dishtowel, and her neglected sauce had stuck to the pan. She had then switched her pan with someone else's and denied this when accused. When Maggie had tried to take her into the corridor to speak to her she'd sworn at her and shot off into the toilets.

'And where is she now?'

'Still in there, locked in.'

'Right-oh. I'll deal with her and let you get back to your class.'

'There is unending variety, not to mention challenge, in this job,' I reflected. 'This morning I was entertaining the local MP and this afternoon I'm prising a reluctant twelve-year-old from a locked toilet.' I sighed resignedly, approaching the toilets.

The girls' ones were bleak but marginally more salubrious than those of the boys. Silence met me as I swung open the door, but Jackie's hiding place was obvious – one cubicle door was closed. This was an occasion for low-key calmness: Jackie had literally got herself into a corner and needed help to get herself out.

'Jackie,' I called, 'it's Miss Smith here. I just want you to come out and tell me what happened.'

After a brief moment the bolt was shot back and a somewhat fearful, but still fierce-faced, Jackie trickled out.

'Why don't you wash your hands and come back with me to the office,' I suggested, and was relieved when she did so without demur. Safely back in my room we sat down to discuss the situation. Apparently Jackie had been bleaching the dishcloths, a job she liked because putting her hands in the bleach removed the nicotine stains from her fingers. Her partner Alison Day, supposed to be stirring the sauce, had burnt it.

'And whose idea was it to switch it?' I asked, knowing how little initiative the colourless Alison ever displayed.

Jackie coloured and looked down. 'Well, it was mine. But she did it.'

'And do you think Mrs Berry was right to blame you?'

'I suppose so,' she admitted reluctantly.

'And what's going to happen now?'

'Oh dinnae tell ma Ma,' she begged. 'She's got a

lot o' worries just now. Please, Ah'll do any thing you want to make up for this.'

'What did your mum do last time, when she was told you'd been smoking?'

'She went mad, and she grounded me. Said she'd put me in a home – but she didnae mean that,' she added quickly.

'What about your dad?'

'Oh she never telt him. He'd have belted me stupid, the same as he does Jimmy when he's been bad.'

In my book the silent Jimmy was so well behaved that this scenario was quite unimaginable, but for the moment I let this pass.

'OK. I'll give you one more chance. You'll go and apologise to Mrs Berry for behaving badly and swearing, and tell her you'll take the punishment you deserve.'

Thankful that her parents were not to be contacted, Jackie went off to meet her doom, and promised to return to let me know what transpired. Maggie Berry's sentence was half an hour's detention every day for a week, when all the sinks, cupboards, and tops in Room B1 would be thoroughly cleaned, along with any pots and dishes left less than clean by other students. The recalcitrant submitted and made the necessary atonement for her sins, but, as I anticipated, more trouble lay ahead.

During the next months there were rumours and rumblings in the staffroom of her doings; complaints about her behaviour in assembly, a bullying incident, and her lack of enthusiasm in class. It all culminated in her being brought to me one day by John Dee, the head of English. When I answered a peremptory knock, I found him on my doorstep with a red-faced Jackie in tow, unsure of whether to be defiant or defensive.

'When her teacher was reprimanding her,' he articulated through gritted teeth, 'this young lady swore disgustingly and shot out of the room, slamming the door on Mrs Black's arm. Her arm is severely bruised, if not broken!'

After a few further well chosen words, detailing what horrors should be inflicted on the girl, he strode off, leaving me to cope. Taking her into my room, I sat her down and for a moment gazed silently at her. This was not what she was expecting and it seemed to unnerve her.

'Ah didnae mean tae hurt her,' she faltered. 'She made me lose ma temper because...'

'Jackie!' I exploded. 'What am I to do with you? You've been in school for only six months, and you've never been off my doorstep!' Again I retreated into silence. My thoughts led me to take a gentler approach. 'I just can't understand you, Jackie. People don't behave like this unless they have problems and are stressed out. Why are you always so angry? Is there something at home that's bothering you?'

I knew my words were hitting home when she dropped her eyes, and started twisting her fingers.

'If there's something wrong you can tell me. I promise you nobody outside this room will hear about it. I just need to know what the problem is in order to understand your behaviour and maybe help you.'

This softer approach disarmed her and she started to cry. She did to control her tears but she had finally cracked, and the hard front she had been maintaining, for years probably, disintegrated. 'It's ma faither,' she gulped, once she could speak. 'Ah hate him! He comes in drunk at night and batters ma mother....' At this she broke down completely, racked with sobs. My heart went out to her, realising the burdens she had been bearing, and the stress she was under. I gave her some tissues, and she accepted a sweetie to help her calm down. After a time she told me more.

'Last night he came in at 1am when we were all in bed, and started shouting at my mum tae get his supper. She told him it was in the oven but she never got up tae get it, so he tipped her out o' bed and kicked her in the face...' Tears fell again as she recalled the horror of it.

'What did you do?' I asked, guessing she would not just be a passive observer.

'I grabbed a vase and hit him on the head while Jimmy ran to the neighbour for help. But ma mother was covered in blood, and we had tae get an ambulance.' She was shaking with horror and rage. 'He knocked out two of her teeth. There was a hole right through her face. They had to operate on her and she's going to be scarred for life,' she wailed despairingly.

'What happened to your dad?' I asked.

'Oh the police took him away for the night, but she'll never make a complaint so they'll never charge him. I hate him! I don't know why she won't leave him. I've asked her often enough!'

'What does she say?'

'She has left him twice but she always goes back. She says it only happens when he's drunk and he's always sorry once he's sober. She says she's nowhere to go, and she's ashamed of what the neighbours will say. That's why Jimmy and I have tae keep quiet about it.' And so saying, she put her head in her hands.

I was heart sorry for her, but having gained these confidences on the promise of confidentiality my hands were tied and I felt fairly helpless. All I could do was provide a listening ear and try to gain sympathy for her from the beleaguered staff to whom she was such a problem – no easy task when they were in the firing line and had no idea of what battles she was fighting at home. My only hope was that I might prove something of a safety valve for her, and, now that she'd shared with me what was at the root of her hostile and disturbed behaviour, her pent up stress and aggression might be lessened.

After a time we discussed what had happened in the English class. She was predictably repentant and, while justice had to be seen to be done, as the phrase goes, I was anxious not to pile further pressure on to this girl.

'Look Jackie,' I said, 'I can understand you were at the end of your tether and couldn't cope with more rows from Mrs Black. I'll try and smooth things over for you, but you'll have to apologise to her and promise to do better.'

'You'll no tell her what Ah told you?' she asked fearfully.

'No,' I promised, 'but I will need to tell her things have been very difficult for you at home – OK?'

'Aye. OK. And thanks,' she replied, even managing a watery smile as I left her to regather her dignity and went off to negotiate peace with Mrs Black. Luckily John Dee's account of Mrs

Black's injuries was exaggerated, and she was still at her post, showing no signs of serious injury. After I explained that it was the stress of an extremely difficult family situation that had caused Jackie to erupt, and that she was now very sorry and willing to accept punishment for what she had done, Mrs Black grudgingly consented to take her back into the class, but she expressed the hope there would be no recurrences. I fervently said amen to that.

Jackie looked more like herself when I reappeared and was glad to hear her apology would be accepted, but I told her that she must come and see me if she ever felt as wound up as that again in order to prevent her getting into further trouble. She agreed and we left things at that.

To expect perfect behaviour from Jackie from then on was unrealistic, and her name still came up in the staffroom conversations, but less frequently, and her wild doings seemed, to me at any rate, to be less serious than previously. I did have to continue making excuses to her teachers for her; however, when our paths crossed I could sense her appreciation that one person at least knew what she was up against.

After returning from a conference where I had picked up a varied collection of leaflets, I decided to seek out Jackie and make a suggestion, so I winkled her out of detention on a Friday afternoon.

'It's OK – you're not in trouble,' I reassured her, as I took her downstairs. 'How's your mother?'

'She's all right,' came the hesitant reply, 'but he's been at it again.'

'Oh dear.... that's too bad.   But I've found something that might interest you, Jackie.'

She perked up as I started rummaging in my filing cabinet.   When I finally found the leaflet I wanted, I drew it out and presented it to her.

'This might help your mum,' I said.   'It's about Women's Aid, an organisation that helps women whose husbands are violent.'

I read through it with her, explaining the concept of Women's Refuges, and the help that was available to battered wives.   Jackie was interested but was reluctant to take the leaflet.

'She'll ken Ah telt you if Ah take that home,' she said.

'Mmm,' I considered.   'Why don't you take it along with a few other social education leaflets, and let her see them?   Maybe she'd be less suspicious.'

'Right,' she said and picked out several others on different topics including AIDS, drug addiction, youth employment and homelessness.   'Ah'll wait till my dad's in the pub and then show her what I got in Social Education and ask her if she wants to read them.   Thanks.'

She carefully pocketed them and then returned resignedly to detention.

I was at an in-service training course on the following Monday, but when I arrived at school on the Tuesday Jackie had beaten me to it and was waiting for me, bright and early.

'You're early,' I remarked.

She smiled. 'I've got good news for you,' she announced. 'Ma dad battered ma mum on Saturday night –'

'Good news, you said?'

'Yes but ma mum left him on Sunday and she says she's never going back!'

'And what about you and Jim?'

'Well Jim couldnae get into the refuge 'cos they don't take boys over twelve, but the Social Work put him with ma auntie just now, and they're goin' tae get my ma a new tenancy, away from HIM!' She was truly excited and I hoped there was going to be a happy ending for her.

Mrs Wright kept her word. After a few days' absence Jackie was back at school. Her housemistress told me that she'd changed her address, and Jimmy was in short term foster care. Eventually they returned to a house in the local area, but at some distance from their previous home. Jackie, of course, didn't suddenly become angelic thereafter but it was a great relief to have better reports about her......and to see a smile on her face when from time to time we came into contact.

Chapter 9

Mothers and Others

When I was young and naive I believed wicked stepmothers were found only in books, but it became clear to me over time that this is not so. Bereavement, broken marriages and cruel step-parents often caused disturbed behaviour and educational failure in young people with the potential to do well if their circumstances had been different.

Kevin was an academically bright young boy whose parents split up just as he was about to enter the High School. This desperate little boy's solution to this problem was to try to blackmail his parents into mending their marriage by refusing to attend school, but predictably, it didn't work. For many months he truanted, stubbornly digging his heels in, until all else having been tried, he had finally to be enrolled in a residential school where he was sadly separated from both of his parents.

Rosie was also a bright girl, with special talents in music and dance; her parents split and she was desperately unhappy when her mother took her and her sister to live with a new partner. An exceptionally strict and truly unpleasant character, he had no time for the new additions to his family and discriminated against them very deliberately. When he bought a new living room carpet Rosie and her sister were forbidden to use it and made to walk on the linoleum surround, while his own children romped around on the new flooring without hindrance. Under a ridiculous regime like this Rosie eventually became anorexic and after months of misery at home and school she eventually had to be taken into foster care.

Andy and Josie had similar problems. When their mother died their father lost no time in remarrying. Unfortunately his new wife already had four children of her own and she blatantly favoured them over her two step-children. They naturally resented having to stand by and watch her buying clothes, sweets and presents for her own youngsters while they were verbally abused and no attempt was made to meet their material or emotional needs.

At one time I was conscious that Josie could profit from having a respite from this negative atmosphere, and was able to arrange for her to go with a friend to a Scripture Union Camp for a short holiday in the summer. Alas, the holiday proved very brief - Josie was sent home after two days for threatening another girl with a knife. This was not her form and I never really got to the bottom of what happened, but I blamed myself for not preparing Josie better for what would be expected of her, and for not briefing beforehand the camp leader who would have been unfamiliar with girls of Josie's ilk.

Andy's resentment of the situation at home was channelled into theft, vandalism and truancy, while Josie's anger was reflected in her rudeness in class, bullying her peers, and disobedience of authority figures. Andy's behaviour led to his being admitted to a school for juvenile offenders, though Josie escaped this by the skin of her teeth.

By the time she was fourteen, our concern, about Josie's behaviour in and out of school and her habitual truancy, led us to refer her to the Children's

Panel – the Scottish equivalent of a juvenile court – on the grounds that she was in need of care. The three-person panel sat on one side of a huge round table with Josie and her father facing them.   At Josie's request I was representing the school and sat on her right, while the assigned social worker, Shona Clarkson, sat to the left of her father. All the panel members had fat files with the family's case history in front of them: Andy had already appeared before the panel several times. They had previously discussed this case and probably made a tentative decision about the outcome.

The chairman, after introducing himself as John Carmichael and naming everyone else, came straight to the point. 'Josie, I see from the school report that you made only 82 attendances out of a possible 151 in the last four months. Is this true?'

She seemed self possessed but she was tight-lipped and I knew she was nervous, dreading the same fate as her brother.

'Aye,' was the succinct reply. She did not intend to be rude, it was just that she knew no better.

Mr Carmichael, well experienced in dealing with monosyllabic unhappy youngsters, gently continued. 'And have you good reasons for being off school so often?'

Fixedly gazing at her fingernails, Josie said very

quietly, 'Not really.'

'Well you know Josie, the law says pupils must attend regularly and can only be excused if they are ill. I wonder what your dad has to say about it all?' he asked, turning to Mr Jackson.

'Ah was fined £20 last year because of her truancy. I've tried ma best,' he said, 'but she just won't go and Ah can hardly stay off work to take her to school,' he responded helplessly.

'Maybe we should ask Josie why she refuses,' suggested the chairman. 'What stops you from going?'

She gave the standard reply to this standard question: 'Ah don't like school.'

How could she explain? She was attempting to draw attention to a multitude of problems in her miserable life: the neglect she suffered, her lack of clothes and money, the impossibility of experiencing normal teenage leisure pursuits, her powerlessness, the irrelevance of school to meet her needs. She did not have the vocabulary, nor the insights to express her gut feelings of hopelessness at the way her life was.... Some, at least, of the panel members would have divined this, but felt there was no value in putting under the microscope the miserable conditions which were the real reason for Josie's opting out of school, and the discussion at the hearing was therefore quite superficial.

Mr Carmichael asked the other two panel members for comments. A sharp-faced older lady, Mrs Duff, took up the challenge. 'What job do you want when you leave school?' she asked.

'Domestic work,' answered Josie.

'Oh, surely you could aim higher than that!' was the dismissive and infuriating reply.

I felt obliged to interject. 'I think that's a realistic ambition for Josie,' I said, and 'I'm sure she'd be very good at it.'

'Yes,' interposed Mr Carmichael, 'and what is the social worker's view?'

'I think Josie could be got back to school if she were placed under supervision and given more encouragement, and I'm sure she'd get a suitable job when she leaves in eighteen months' time,' said Shona.

'Ah yes', said the chairman,' you haven't long to go now, have you? Do you think you could make a big effort and give the school another try if we all rallied round to support you?' he asked, smiling.

Realising her 'sentence' was probably going to be lighter than expected, Josie's face cracked into a smile, and she muttered, 'Aye, maybe.'

Once further discussion had taken place and the Panel's decision was confirmed, to place Josie under Social Work supervision and provide the Panel with six monthly updates on her progress, we were free to go. (The Reporter, whose job is to head up the Children's Panel, was sympathetic when I later complained about Mrs Duff's snobbish and inappropriate remark, and promised to take it further.)

In the months ahead, helped by social work intervention and with the support of a tolerant staff, Josie did hold things together at school well enough to finish the course, albeit without academic distinction, and she embarked on domestic work as she had planned.

Twenty years later in a local supermarket I was vainly trying to reach an item on the top shelf when a male customer helpfully accessed it for me. When I turned round I was surprised to be addressed by Josie who was his companion. After greeting me and reminding me of who she was, she introduced me as 'Isobel' to this person who turned out to be her husband! I was really glad to see that she seemed happy, and to hear she was successfully bringing up a family, including a lovely four-year-old who was with them.

There is no substitute for good parenting and nothing can compensate if it is missing.

One mother, an alcoholic, was usually senseless from drink by mid-afternoon. Somehow her husband seemed to hold things together and the three older children, all of whom had some academic ability, managed to survive school though each seemed to have a chip on the shoulder and often clashed with authority; they were the kind of youngsters who, along with their teachers, breathe sighs of relief when they attain the school leaving age.

The fourth child was disruptive from the word go: her features seemed to suggest foetal alcohol syndrome, and it was quite likely her older siblings had been responsible for her upbringing. Since she had obviously always been accustomed to having her own way and had never learned to knuckle under or accept no for an answer, she had been given the worst possible preparation for adulthood, and had no hope of lasting the course in an institution which, however sympathetic it was to youngsters with problems, nevertheless required basic discipline and respect for authority. Katie was a very angry child, in constant conflict with her teachers. She struggled in mainstream, frequently being suspended for her defiance and disobedience, until finally, when she was in danger of permanent exclusion, she was placed in a small alternative school which provided a more flexible regime and the individual attention she needed. She continued to be demanding and disobedient but her behaviour was more easily tolerated in a small group and once she learned some respect for her teacher she did knuckle under to some extent, and even accepted discipline from time to time. By the time she reached sixteen, the school leaving age, though her social skills were minimal she was literate and numerate; but love and discipline having been sadly lacking throughout her life, she was ill prepared for the adult world. Like many others with similar backgrounds she drifted into drink and drugs, and we were very saddened when we heard some years later that she had taken her own life in a women's prison.

Chapter 10

Ups and Downs, but Mostly Downs

No sooner had we arrived at Fortingall Youth Hostel for a 5 day field trip than I noticed 'JUMBO' scrawled, in big black letters, on the stair wall. This was horrifying because I could guess who was responsible, and could not afford to lose the goodwill of the warden. I immediately confronted Jumbo, the large disaffected autographer, and his reply was predictable.

'It wisnae me,' he growled, angrily towering over me.

Only too aware of the boy's potential but filled with the courage of my convictions I stood my ground, inwardly quaking but knowing this battle had to be won.

'Either you scrub this off right now, or you get into the minibus and we take you home.'

I fully intended to carry out this threat and I think he knew it. He did make a half hearted attempt to stare me down. Then he decided to lose face rather than forfeit a week away, so much to my relief he did the necessary clean up.

Two thirteen year old boys in my English class had been so impertinent that even their classmates were shocked, and the tawse, commonly in use in Scottish schools at that time, seemed an appropriate punishment. The first boy held out his hand as directed and took his one stroke of the belt without batting an eyelid. But the second boy was clearly frightened. He was a lad who had once informed the class that he was 'only the size o' a pint bottle' when he was born; he was certainly very small for his age, and wearing a shirt much too large for him. A pantomime followed as a silent class watched. Slowly and carefully he unrolled the sleeves until the cuffs completely covered his hands. Three times he held out his sleeve-covered hand and three times he pulled it back while the class looked on with interest.

I felt such a brute; but I had to mount a face saving operation and resolve the situation so I ordered him to come out into the corridor.

'Jamie,' I said, 'You and Dod were very cheeky and you have to take your punishment. Dod took his so you have to as well.'

'If ye let me off Ah'll no dae it again,' he promised. Then he folded his arms defensively.

'Tell you what,' I suggested, 'if you hold out your hand I'll just give you a wee tap and I promise it won't be hard.'

He summoned up his courage and held out his hand so that the class, listening intently inside, heard him take one stroke of the belt and believed honour was satisfied.

I had a revelation that day: I realised that being a guidance teacher and counsellor was incompatible with corporal punishment, and I never resorted to it again.

Part of my role involved developing the Community Service course where each student had a half, or even a whole day, doing practical work. The placements could be at the Dog and Cat Home or local pre-school playgroups, and some were with elderly or handicapped people. At the beginning of the session the whole class did group visits to various establishments before being given individual placements and it was an eye-opener to see deprived youngsters, with apparently little to offer, responding to needy people whether disabled, blind, elderly, mentally handicapped or very young.

One small and undernourished fourteen year old boy who had rarely found success in any school subject was an inspiration. On a visit to a small unit of severely disabled primary aged children in Gogarburn he was targeted by a little girl who rolled a ball towards him; he responded appropriately by sitting on the floor beside her and rolling it back. Thrilled, she held his hand as we walked around the unit and showed disappointment when we had to go. Having made a hit he was delighted when he was granted his request for a placement there, and his school attendance improved remarkably, especially on Wednesdays, which he never missed. Another similar boy was placed in the Royal Blind School. On his return from his first spell I asked him how it had gone.

'It was rubbish!' was his reply and in the same breath he said, 'Can Ah go again next week?'

Some classes we dreaded teaching but the

philosophy adopted by the new regime was that the staff was a team and had to support one other. One class of fifteen year old boys became increasingly problematic as their leaving age drew near and their struggling English teacher was delighted to exchange them for easier classes three hours a week. It was my privilege to have them for one of these hours, in a music room containing two grand pianos; I have to confess that the prospect of taking them robbed me of my appetite for lunch on Tuesday afternoons, as I summoned all my energies for the task ahead. Luckily the classroom was surrounded by small empty music practice rooms so I could operate a 'divide and rule' strategy where anyone too outrageous was ordered to leave the large class and work alone in a little room, without an audience.

On one occasion a particularly tough boy who had offended beyond what could be tolerated refused to leave, and worse still, told me to 'Go to hell!'

Infuriated and totally determined he would immediately reap the punishment he deserved, I demanded that he accompany me to visit the Head. Amazingly he meekly followed me as I left the room. I had not made an idle threat and the Head, true to his philosophy, supported me to the hilt, demanding an apology first and then sending for the boy's parents. I scurried quickly back to the classroom where, surprisingly, mayhem had not broken out, perhaps because the rest of them were waiting for the axe to fall also on them.

Occasions like this were few and far between but very sapping of one's strength and a dreadful waste of teaching time.

Learning outside the classroom through visits, practical work and outdoor pursuits was the order of the day. One keen young biologist took a group of tough boys to the Union Canal to net specimens which they would examine under binocular microscopes. When a body was found in the water even these hardened delinquents were shaken; they had to summon their normal enemy, the police, for help. When the sergeant began asking them questions they felt less than comfortable and eventually one witness, asked for his name and address, protested, and questioned the need to divulge this.

'Well,' replied the po-faced bobby, 'surely you know if you report a find to the police you get it back if it isn't claimed!'

Foolishly, with hindsight, just as their leaving date approached, we took half a dozen difficult boys to a tumbledown cottage in the Queen Elizabeth Forest for a two day trip. We had to go where vandalism would be no problem and there were no neighbours to disturb, so the venue was remote, and facilities were minimal. As there was no electricity, in the evening we were enjoying sitting in the living space around a big log fire, making toast and drinking cocoa when one boy appeared in great distress, brandishing his new leather jacket which had been maliciously cut to ribbons by one of his envious 'pals'. Two culprits were identified and about to be driven straight home, when they ran off in the dark into the woods. Anxious for their safety when they had not returned by ten o'clock, we phoned to ask the local police for help in finding them but by the time they located us in the heart of the forest the boys had returned and were prowling round outside the cottage. Terrified in the black darkness, they were easily persuaded to get into the school minibus to be driven home to civilisation.

Seeing it was one lone woman proposing to transport the delinquents on the two hour journey home, one burly policeman expressed some anxiety.

'Are ye sure ye'll be a'richt?' he enquired.

'Oh yes,' I replied. 'They've lost their stuffing.'

We were all right (discounting running out of petrol at midnight and having to find an all night garage that would take my debit card) and each boy was deposited at his home around one in the morning, with a minimal explanation to his parents and instructions to report to the Head at nine in the morning.

After a short night in my own bed I called the Head very early to brief him on the situation and set off for the cottage to arrive in time to have breakfast with the remnant.

That was by no means our finest hour.

The following episode was stressful at the time but looking back one has to laugh.

The Head decided to accompany a group of S6 students on a visit to Atlantic College in Wales, for a five day trip, taking one of the three assistant heads with him. The Depute Head along with two other Assistant Headteachers would be ably coping in their absence.

Unfortunately on the first day the Deputy was struck down by a virus, and the next day the other AHT put out a disc in his back, so for three days I was on my own, doing the work normally done by five people. This involved arranging cover daily for absent teachers, teaching my own classes, disciplining students referred to the hierarchy, interviewing parents and other callers, keeping going the guidance programme and responding to all the usual unexpected demands which arose.

I did send a telegram to the two layabouts in Wales with an anguished appeal which read 'Come back you rats – the ship is sinking!' But the reply I got was worded, 'Send more golf balls! Heidie.'

At the end of one dreadful day when absolutely everything had gone pear-shaped, I was sitting in my office totally drained when the Head burst in.

'A girl from X School was loitering in A Block and shot into the girls' toilets when I challenged her! I want you to get her and take her to the police station!' he demanded and then, typically, disappeared.

Dutifully but somewhat apprehensively, I made my way to the battlefield, and surprised myself by my success in winkling her out without any manhandling, and persuading her to be driven to the local police station. Though the police were somewhat taken aback by this unaccustomed demand I was able just to explain her trespass to them and leave her there to be dealt with.

This event is indelibly fixed in my memory: on the way home I stopped at a photo booth to be photographed for my bus pass which, forever after, depicted me as dull-eyed, exhausted and strained to the limit!

The school reacted very positively to a stray tabby cat which decided to make its home in the school: she was officially adopted and made much of, but sadly towards the end of the term she disappeared, after a lengthy stay, and we were all disappointed.

At the end of the long summer holidays, on our return to school, we were horrified when the janitor revealed that the cat had eventually been found drowned, in the cold water cistern. It was said that this tank was the source of the staffroom water supply, used to make the coffee and tea that we all drank daily!

Teachers have to be tough, but even the toughest have their moments of terror. On one occasion I was standing in for the teacher who ran our small group of P7 boys whose behaviour we were attempting to modify, to allow them to fit in when they enrolled at the high school. As the school day was finishing, Bert, a seriously disturbed boy provoked beyond endurance by a classmate, suddenly swore, pushed over his desk and ran out into the small room next door. I went after him, but not before sending a 'trustie' downstairs for help.

Bert was standing in a corner facing me, with fists clenched, and completely beside himself. Breathing hard he picked up a chair as if to use it as a weapon, so closing the door behind me to exclude an aggravating audience, I spoke very quietly, my heart in my mouth.

'Bert, put it down and don't be silly.'

'Let me oot!' he yelled. 'Ah'm gaun hame!'

Outwardly calm but inwardly quaking and expecting the chair to be hurled at me, I spoke.

'Just wait a bit and calm down,' I said quietly. 'You can't go home like that.'

A short stand-off followed during which I contemplated my next move, praying for help. And then a miracle occurred. Bert's mother who had never before come to pick him up arrived at that moment with the downstairs teacher. I shook with relief. He completely changed as his mother asked what he thought he was doing and demanded that he apologise. We quickly bade them goodbye, dismissed the other lads, and then collapsed in the staffroom for a reviving cup of tea.

Towards the end of June I accompanied four girls on a weekend expedition to Barnes Youth Hostel to practise for their Duke of Edinburgh expedition. On the Saturday, having done all our map work, we set out to walk across the hills from Stobo to Drummelzier Glen. Climbing up towards Whitelaw and Pykestone Hills on a hot June day was quite a struggle, and though we took it gently up the ridge we were drenched in sweat when we reached the top. However, up there we felt as if we were on the top of the world and we were rewarded by magnificent views of the Southern Uplands in every direction. After an unforgettable picnic in the heather we strolled along the tops for an hour, before reluctantly making our way down the glen from Toberon Law and then taking the long hard road home to the hostel.

When it finally came into view we were feeling very dry, hot and dusty and temptation struck. The River Lyne ran, cool and inviting, through glorious green fields bordered by trees newly in leaf; no one was in sight for miles. Undeterred by lack of swimming kit and towels, each of us retired to undress modestly behind our own private bush and then slipped into the water, wearing only bra and pants. It was such a treat to bathe in cool, clean river water and wash off the sweat and dust of the day! The discomfort of negotiating the last few fields, just sundried and without our underwear, mattered not at all.

Chapter 11

Trip of a Lifetime

Friday came round very fast, and I was yet again about to take a group away for the weekend. Rounding the corner laden with daysacks and sleeping bags, I narrowly avoided a collision with Mrs Weir.

'Oh, that was close!' she gasped, as she regained her balance. 'But you're just the person I'm wanting to see!'

We were quite well acquainted through playing

bingo at the Parents' Association, and I knew Mrs Weir as a great wee woman who did her best with the little she had and was always ready for a laugh.

'Come on then,' I encouraged her. 'We'll go and have a seat in my office – that's where I'm taking all this stuff.'

As we sat down I could see she was ill at ease and twisting a screw of paper in her hands.

'What can I do for you?' I asked.

Looking a little flushed, she began to explain. 'Well, Ah hate tae say this – but, well, money's very difficult the now. Ma man's no workin' and we're on benefits. And that disnae amount tae much...'

'I know,' I sympathised, 'and what can we help you with?'

'Ah'm worried because Nancy's been off school all week.'

'Well. It happens,' I said. 'You never keep her off unless she's ill.'

'Aye. That's the problem. She's no ill...'

'Oh dear, it's not like her to play truant!' I responded.

'Oh, she's no truanting – it's just that she hasnae any shoes and we've nae money tae buy any.' She was thoroughly embarrassed, but having begun her story she ploughed on relentlessly. 'We've just enough for food and coal, and there's nothing for extras. Look at this.' She unscrewed her scrap of paper and held it out. On the back of an envelope she had neatly detailed her meagre income and the family's weekly outgoings, with costs: breakfast cereal, milk, beans, potatoes, bread, marge, jam, sausages, pies, teabags, corned beef.... they clearly survived on cheap, filling food with no treats.

'Turn over and you'll see the coal and electricity payments.'

I, in my turn, was embarrassed to see Mrs W. brought to the point of what could only be described as begging. I knew only desperation could do this.

'Ma man's on the dole. We don't buy fags or drink, like some. That's our weekly expenses, and there's nothing to spare for things like shoes...'

She sat with her hands on her knees, not meeting my eyes. 'Ah've heard you can apply for a grant,' she said.

'Yes, you can', I replied, 'and I'll give you the form right now. But it usually takes weeks before the vouchers come through, and Nancy can't wait that long.'

'But what else can I do?' she asked despairingly.

'I'll get the school welfare assistant to take Nancy out to get some trainers, and they'll keep her going meantime,' I offered.

'Well, Ah'm grateful for the offer, but Ah'll never

be able to repay you...'

'No, no,' I protested, 'you must look on this as a gift out of school funds – money you've helped to raise yourself! We do use it like this from time to time – but keep quiet about it or everybody will be asking!'

I was trying to ease her discomfort by joking about it, though it was no joke. I knew, from experience, of pupils kept at home for weeks for lack of clothes and shoes, and we habitually bought what they needed to cut the red tape which caused delays.

Mrs W. was happy to accept the offer when it was put this way, and even happier to keep quiet about it. She wasn't one of those who gloated about how much they could screw out of the system – on the contrary, she would hate anyone to know she'd accepted charity.

'Now mind and fill in the forms,' I told her. 'It will take a while but Nancy will eventually get some good shoes, and maybe a jacket as well.'

Thanking me profusely, she promised to return the forms. For some antiquated reason, grants for clothing came out of a police fund, and I forbore to tell her she would have to go to a police depot to collect the shoes. I had previously been appalled to read, in the literature about this charitable fund set up in the Victorian era, that donors to the fund were invited to attend sessions to view the 'needy children' receiving the benefits they had condescended to provide. I only hoped this circus was no longer in operation in more enlightened modern times.

As she went out, wending her way through heaps of cagoules, wellies and suchlike, she remarked on what was on view. 'Ye've enough stuff here for an army! Are ye goin' away on a trip?'

'I sure am!' I laughed. 'I'm off to Aviemore with my SU Club for the weekend.'

'Lucky you!' was her response. 'Ah wish it was me! We never – '

'No, we didn't,' I interrupted, 'but times have changed!'

'Aye,' she sighed, 'they certainly have!'

No doubt she'd have loved a break. A weekend away from her pressing problems must have seemed very inviting to her, though to me the prospect of yet again taking a rowdy group to the Highlands for two days was somewhat daunting, after another busy and exhausting week. Sometimes I wondered why I did it. It couldn't have happened without my helpers, the local assistant minister Ally and his wife Babs, and a young teacher Rachel. They were all full of energy and enthusiasm.

As she made her way homewards I returned to my preparations. We were used to doing everything on the cheap, and it was good to know this annual trip was largely funded by a £400 grant from Children in Need.   It let us rent accommodation a little better than the very basic outdoor centres we were used to, and, instead of having to think up and prepare for interesting activities that cost nothing, we could offer our deprived urban youngsters opportunities to do things normally right out of their reach. This meant less work and more fun for the staff, too.

On a Friday school finished early, and all too soon our excited mob was clustering round the minibus, clamouring to go. Everyone conversed in loud shouts while Rachel collected the five pound fee that most, though not all of them, had managed to raise.

'Hey, Miss, can Ah sit in the front seat?' asked Lee, always with an eye to the main chance.

'Well, yes, but somebody else will have to get their turn at Perth,' I decreed.

This seat was much in demand and we always tried to make sure there was no favouritism. My three helpers were shoehorning everyone in, along with their luggage and an extraordinary medley of items: tinned soup, cornflakes, a guitar, maps and cagoules, to name a few. As usual, every conversation was conducted in loud shouts.

'Put your bags under the seats,' yelled Ally, 'and

keep your swimming trunks out!'

'Great!' bellowed Stu. 'Are we swimming in Perth Pool?'

'Aye!' was Mac's shouted reply. 'We got telt that on Tuesday!'

'Oh, Miss,' wailed Sean, 'Ah've forgotten ma trunks!'

'Never mind,' was Ally's reply. 'We'll hire some for you.'

Eventually everyone was seated and we sped off to the Bridge to try to beat the Friday traffic jam.

Teenage boys aren't the most hygienic of creatures and it was a relief to get out into the fresh air after an hour cooped up with them in the minibus. Our policy to take them swimming at the start of every trip effectively diminished their body odours and also helped to rid them of some of their excessive energy. Immediately we drew up at Perth Pool, the boys were out of the van and elbowing their way through the crowd, before we could call them back.

'Leaders first!' shouted Ally. 'We've got the money! Anyway, you've forgotten to lock the windows! And don't leave any valuables in the bus!' The last injunction was fairly irrelevant, but they did have some things they didn't want to lose.

'Aye,' said Bry, 'last year somebody broke the windae and stole ma liquorice allsorts!'

'Yes,' said Mac, 'and they – '

'Now look,' interrupted Babs forcefully, 'I don't want any of you lot giving us a red face in here. Calm down and try to behave like normal human beings!'

'Cheek,' grinned Dave, but Ally's wife Babs, though heavily pregnant, easily commanded their respect, and they usually did as she asked.

'The sooner they dispose of their energy the quicker,' muttered Rachel breathlessly as we trotted up the ramp after them.

Finally, we all made it into the pool, happy that the wave machine came on just as we were about to jump in. As we only had an hour, everyone spent the time excitedly haring from the flumes, to the river rapids, to the jacuzzi, to the bubble beds and so forth, until all too soon it was time to go. Hunger pangs lured us out and back to the chipshop where our pre-ordered suppers were waiting; after making short work of those and several bottles of cola we were soon back on the road north, and by seven-thirty we reached our destination, a pleasant Outdoor Centre near Aviemore.

After a short period of exploration and settling into the dormitories, we consumed our supper: tomato soup and mountains of buttered toast. The boys weren't fussy about the food they ate as long as it was familiar and plentiful. For several of them, having plenty was quite a novelty, and for all of them escaping from the urban ghetto where they lived, even briefly, was a delight; it was a pleasure for the leaders that they rarely complained and appreciated the small luxuries they weren't used to.

After lying around the lounge watching a lengthy James Bond video, most people settled down for the night, though poor Ally was forced to drag his mattress through to sleep on the floor of the noisiest dorm. However, by midnight everyone had succumbed to sleep.

Saturday was hectic. First we enjoyed the high skywalk in Carrbridge among the pine trees at Landmark, and then the adventure park in the woods with its unforgettable chute. Even I was forcibly prevailed upon to clamber to the top and then plummet down this terrifyingly vertical tube. Catapulted out at the bottom, I struggled feebly to my feet. 'That was ghastly! Never again!' I declared, and I sincerely meant it.

This contrasted sharply with the reaction of the boys who, yelling appreciation as they exited, without exception leapt smartly to their feet and raced back for another go.

Once the park's attractions had been fully sampled we made for the Go-Karting Centre at Aviemore and excitedly queued for a good half hour in order to spend five minutes – and five pounds each – hurtling round the track in pseudo racing cars. Luckily the karts' highest speed was restricted, but the boys, at an age when they were desperate to drive, feverishly sped round at the absolute maximum, wearing racing goggles and helmets, and fancying themselves as Formula Oners. The rules forbidding racing and bumping were conveniently ignored, as all of them strove to get their full money's worth. Their five minute turns were short, though one or two managed to produce money of their own to pay for a second round.

'Ah've got ma granny tae thank for that,' smiled Gary, one of the lucky few. 'She gi'ed me a fiver off her pension!'

Saturday evening was taken up by a talent contest. Divided into four groups, the boys had to prepare one or two items which would be performed as part of a concert programme. The motivating prize was a huge cake, baked by Rachel whose cooking was legendary, and so competition was fierce.

Normally the boys got on well, though there was the usual amount of rivalry and teasing when sometimes things went too far. Unfortunately this happened during our preparations for the contest. Lee sat down on a rotten banana placed in his sleeping bag by Sean, and was not amused. Words were followed by punches after which Lee shot out into the darkness.   As I rehearsed a skit with my group Sean and Eric interrupted.

'Miss, Lee's run away in a rage! He says he's goin' home!'

'Oh no,' I groaned. This wasn't the first time Lee had reacted like this. He usually came back once he cooled down, but we couldn't leave him out there in pitch darkness in unfamiliar forest territory.

With Sean and Eric beside me I drove slowly down the narrow rutted track and eventually spotted the hunched figure trudging along. We stopped and invited him into the van, only to be subjected to a mouthful of foul abuse.

'Oh Miss!' said a shocked Eric, under the impression I had never before been exposed to such language.

We drove on past looking for a turning place, and then went back to renew our offer but Lee's temper had not abated, and he again refused.

'OK Lee,' I said, but I can't leave you here – I'll have to call the police.'

'Phone the f---ing polis if you like!' raged Lee. 'Ah'm walkin' hame!'

I could do nothing without his co-operation and left him there meantime as we returned to the centre. I had every intention of calling the police but just as we got back I was urgently summoned by my group whose turn it was to perform, and so I attended to them first. I was pleased to see them perform well, and even more pleased to hear Rachel's whisper just afterwards that Lee had come back on his own. As the concert proceeded Ally spoke lengthily with Lee, calling his bluff and offering to take him home, but Lee apologised and the matter was closed when he and Sean finally made up.

My group was awarded a third of the cake for coming second in the contest but they and the winners kindly donated one slice each to everyone else at suppertime, so no one lost out entirely. Following evening prayers everyone fell into bed and after a day of perpetual motion there were no high jinks on the programme this second night.

Next morning we successfully ran our own 'church' service with a difference. There was only one hitch during the prayers when Hendo prayed that Babs's bairn, due soon, 'would come oot a' richt', and everyone dissolved into laughter. He was not praying about the actual birth but was trying to articulate his hopes that the baby would be whole and healthy, and a credit to its parents, but everyone was amused at how he worded this. However, the laugh over, we all settled down and the short service continued to its end.

As we were packing up to go, Joe asked to speak to me. We drew aside, and, very embarrassed, he explained that he'd wet the bed. We discreetly let the housekeeper know and she promised to deal with it. I was thankful Joe had told me – once before in the Borders there had been a similar occurrence when the bed-wetter just turned over the mattress and left without confessing; following this I'd been upset to receive a cleaning bill along with a nasty letter from the warden.

We had two last treats on the way home: a visit to the Highland Wildlife Park followed by a meal in the Little Chef Restaurant at Killiecrankie. The boys loved the wildlife park, but the dinner was a special treat as their experience of eating out was mostly limited to carry-outs, and now they were having waitress service! Everyone was allowed five pounds worth of food from the menu, and each one pored over the menu, determined to exploit this chance to the full! Most of them went for quantity, and chose custom cooked all-day breakfasts, followed by an ice cream dessert. After lingering over this experience we eventually reeled back to the minibus, very replete and ready to sleep for the rest of the journey.

Alas, no weekend could be perfect: as we headed for home, Gary somehow managed to put his elbow through the van's back window, causing it to leave its frame and crash on to the road. He was unhurt but justice demanded a punishment and he was sentenced to walk the last three miles of the journey home. This episode woke the sleeping Dave and Joe, napping beside me in the front.

'This trip's cost a bomb,' said Dave, 'a lot more than a fiver!'

'That's why the school's always raising money,' I explained.

'You mean the school paid for a' that?' asked Joe.

'No. It did pay some. But most of the treats were paid because I got a grant from a trust.'

'Great!' said Lee who was eavesdropping. 'Can we do it again next year?'

Chapter 12

Comfort Eating

Curiously, Jo rang from the primary school just as I was about to phone her.

'Hullo!' I exclaimed. 'I was on the point of ringing you! We must be telepathic.'

'In that case you won't need to guess what my call's about,' she replied.

'I expect it'll be the Dunn family.'

'Quite right! It is.'

It was not surprising we were on the same wavelength, catering as we did for families who had children in both primary and secondary schools.

We often shared our concerns when family upsets affected children's behaviour and sometimes we worked together over pupils' problems.

'OK. You talk first,' I said.

'Right,' said Jo. 'We have a small girl, Ella, that we really worry about. Her attendance is poor and when she does come she can't get enough to eat and her clothes are a disgrace. Not only that but today her wee sister, Georgie, arrived very upset with a cut on her hand. She said her mother had done it but that is hard to believe. Have you something to add to this?'

'Well Janice's tutor's been worried about her for a while. But recently things have got worse. Today she turned up in the freezing cold wearing only a short-sleeved T-shirt and shorts. When her tutor made a remark about it she started to cry. She said she had had a coat on when she left the house but her mother had dragged it off her back and kept it.'

'Why on earth would she do that?'

'Janice said her ma was in a bad mood and wanted her to stay at home and keep her company.'

'Oh dear,' said Jo, 'it seems as if there's more to this than meets the eye. Maybe we need to meet and discuss this. What do you think?'

I arranged to meet Jo in her office at the end of the school day, when we could talk without interruption over a coffee. As we shared our thoughts it became clear the Dunn girls were having a hard time and some action was needed. In common with seventy per cent of our pupils all three had free school lunches, and the High School also provided the older girl with breakfast, when she came, but their clothing and shoes were pitifully inadequate, and all three were becoming very angry little girls, swearing and hitting out on the least provocation. Neither of us had met the mother but in our locality that was not unusual: lots of our parents, having had unhappy school experiences themselves, viewed schools as unsympathetic places and fought shy of them. After deciding we didn't have sufficient grounds for a referral to the Children's Panel, Jo and I decided our first call should be to the Social Work Department. There and then Jo phoned the duty officer and I sat listening to a one-sided conversation.

'Hello – Jo Clarke, head of Garth Primary here. I'd like to speak to the duty officer please,' she said.

'Oh good!' She gave me the thumbs up. 'It's Julie Henderson – she's just...' She was interrupted.

'Hi Julie! Jo Clarke here.'

Julie's words were indecipherable.

'Yes,' was Jo's reply, 'we're doing overtime, as usual.'

More from Julie.

'No this won't take long, I hope. Do you have the Dunn family of 45 Eastmuir Avenue on your books?'

A short reply from Julie.

'Fine,' said Jo, turning to me. 'She's gone to check,' explained Jo, and we hadn't long to wait for the reply which was very short.

'Oh really,' was Jo's answer.' Thanks very much. We'll contact them then.'

More muttering from the other end.

'No, lucky you! This is not your problem, but thanks anyway. Bye just now.'

Putting down the phone Jo explained that this family had had long term problems and they were receiving support from the Family Service Unit. This was good news because the FSU, an independent social work organisation, took on only a limited case load and provided extensive long term support to seriously needy families. The regular social work department was often overwhelmed by referrals and could usually only undertake crisis intervention when families or individuals were at desperation point. It was good to know the FSU were already aware of this family, and Jo and I were confident they could provide the help needed.

I agreed to make the call to the FSU the next morning. Sharing confidential information was always difficult but, knowing two of the team quite well, I was able to get the chance to discuss our concerns with Lesley, whom I'd worked with before.

'Yeah,' said Lesley, 'we've also been a bit worried about Mrs Dunn. She came around a lot earlier in the year but recently we've seen very little of her, and she's seemed very trauchled, but unwilling to say why. I had the impression her marriage was faltering, and she said she was looking for a job.'

'Maybe there's been some kind of crisis this week,' I suggested. 'Georgie and Janice were both quite distressed yesterday when they turned up at their schools'.

'If wee Georgie's been hurt by her mother and Janice's had her coat pulled off,' said Lesley, 'that is really serious. Maybe we need to call a quick conference of everyone involved, in order to get the whole picture.'

After further discussion we decided this was the way to go and an emergency case conference was set for the next morning.

I arrived early in the Family Service Unit, closely followed by Josh Berger, a highly respected local doctor, and then Jo turned up with her school nurse and also Alan Pope, an educational psychologist who knew each of the girls. As we sipped at our tea it occurred to me that along with Lesley and her senior,

Wilma Laing, this was quite a forbidding group. Mrs Dunn, when she came in with Lesley and Wilma, clearly agreed, for she was visibly trembling and unable to look anyone in the eye. Lesley helped her to a seat, provided her with a cuppa and cheerfully introduced us all to each other, but this did little to lighten the strained atmosphere.

Wilma, after making all the introductions, asked Lesley to open the meeting.

'Mrs Dunn says things have been very hard lately,' Lesley began,' and I've explained to her that one or two of us have been a bit worried about the children. I called this meeting so we could talk about what extra help the family needs through this difficult time.'

Then she asked Jo to explain why she and her staff were concerned.

Jo, ill at ease, glanced at the mother and told how the school nurse's report that the girls were seriously underweight together with the girls' aggressive behaviour and frequent absences had led to a referral to the psychologist. Mr Pope told how Mrs Dunn had permitted this because her girls though bright were under-achieving, and everyone was working to change this.

'And I think there was an incident yesterday.....?' prompted Wilma.

'Well,' said Jo, hesitantly glancing again towards Mrs Dunn who was now shaking like a leaf, 'yesterday we had to strap up a cut on Georgie's hand. She said her mother had done it with a knife!'

Mrs Dunn seemed to flinch, and Lesley put an arm round the back of her chair at this point.

Wilma intervened with '– and the High School teachers were unhappy too, Miss Smith?'

'Yes,' I answered, feeling on the spot and unwilling to add to this poor woman's pain. 'Janice told her tutor that before she left yesterday morning you had pulled her coat off her back, because you wanted her to stay in the house.'

Mrs Dunn's face crumpled as she made to respond. But at that point Dr Berger intervened.

'Maybe I need to say something now. Mrs Dunn has given me permission to explain some of her difficulties. You should know she's had serious debt problems and is on drugs for clinical depression. She also finds it hard to be alone all day, and now that their dad has left the children are behaving badly.'

'Aye,' she broke in, 'Ah'm at my wits' end wi' them!'

'We know that, Mamie,' said Lesley, 'but what's all this about Georgie's cut hand, and you keeping Janice's coat?'

'Since ma man left last month they've been

running wild and jist won't take a telling,' she faltered. 'Ah was desperate no tae be left alone yesterday but Janice wouldnae stay. Georgie wanted tae take that knife tae school for craft work. It was far too sharp but she was determined. When Ah tried tae grab it off her the blade cut the back o' her hand...'

While she mopped her eyes, Wilma briefly summed up the situation. 'Well Mamie, we can see you're at rock bottom just now, but you can see why everyone's concerned for the girls.'

'Aye, but so am I! They're ma bairns and Ah dinnae want them taken away fae me!'

Lesley passed a tissue to Mamie, now weeping unrestrainedly. Probably in common with everyone else in the group, I felt highly uncomfortable taking part in this charade. This poor woman was really up against it, her life falling apart, and here we were adding fuel to the fire.

'We haven't seen you for ages,' said Wilma quietly. 'I wish you'd –'

'How could Ah come and tell ye what happened! Ma man spending every ha'penny on booze and then leaving me for a prostitute!'

She sat despairingly with her hands over her eyes, and it seemed to me that a blanket of gloom descended on all of us. Lesley proposed a brief interval to help her become calmer. In the ten minutes before we resumed fresh coffee was served, people stretched their legs, and two of the group went out for a quick smoke. I wished I too had the means of dispelling the tense knot in my diaphragm. Time was passing and there was so much waiting to be done back at school.

'Gosh, Jo,' I murmured, 'wouldn't it be great to have something right now that calmed you down and also pepped you up!'

'Oh, that's called alcohol,' she laughed. 'Unfortunately not on offer at present!'

Quite quickly, it seemed, the group reconvened, and business resumed.   During the break Wilma and Lesley had chatted with Mamie, who seemed more in control now, and Lesley said she wanted to say something.

'Go on then Mamie,' Lesley encouraged her.

'Ah just wanted tae say Ah know Ah'm not perfect, but I do want to be a good mother and please don't suggest taking the kids into care.'

Wilma explained we weren't at that point yet, but some assurances were needed from Mrs Dunn so she and the children could get out of the hole they were in.

'Like what?' said the mother.

'We need you to let us help with debt management, and we'd like you here at the Mums'

Club two or three times a week at least,' said Wilma.

'Aye, that's fine. Ah'd like that,' she said.

'And we think it would help if the girls came here after school each day. That way they could get help with their homework , and we could keep an eye on them.'

'Aye, that's fine,' she said again, seeming relieved.

'Has anyone else something to suggest, or a question?' asked Wilma, looking round the group.

'Perhaps a week away quite soon might help the family?' suggested Dr Berg.

Mrs Dunn visibly brightened.

'Yes, that's a possibility,' responded Lesley. 'The Mums' group are going off to Haggerston for five days at the October break.'

Jo and I both chipped in to ask if the girls could all have financial assistance to go on school trips coming up later in the term, and Lesley agreed to pursue this. I sensed the atmosphere lightening.

'Well maybe we can sum up now,' said Wilma finally. 'The family are going to see more of us at the unit, most of us have a better grasp of what has caused the problems we've seen, and all of us, including Mamie, will work together to improve things. Anything you want to add, Mamie?'

Clearly relieved her ordeal was over, Mamie even seemed glad at the outcome.

'No really. Just thank you,' she said, gathering her coat round her as she prepared to leave.

The rest of us took our cue and made our goodbyes without delay, aware as I was that their presence was already in demand elsewhere. Immensely relieved it was all over, I felt my tense muscles relaxing, and I had a desperate craving for food. I was only too aware of my problems: the school lunch break was almost over, I was too late for school dinners and I hadn't brought my usual packed lunch. I shot off to the local baker's to buy something to eat in the staffroom in the last minutes of the lunch hour. Predictably, as I wolfed down my goodies, my colleagues subjected me to a barrage of criticism.

'Sausage rolls? What's happened to the raw carrots?' asked one.

I loftily ignored this but more followed.

'Cream cookies! I thought these were proscribed,' laughed Meg.

'They're PREscribed, for stress,' I muttered through a mouthful, 'and highly effective. Have one,' I offered.

Meg feigned horror. 'How can you? We've got Weightwatchers tonight! Are you going to confess to the cream cookies?'

'If you'd spent this past hour as I have you'd be comfort eating too,' I complained, stuffing in the second cookie. 'I should get danger money! I'll never be thin as long as I'm in this job!'

Chapter 13

A Bunny and a Barbecue

In June, things often became quiet after many of our sixteen year olds had left school to enter the world of work or go to college, and as the long holidays approached attendance dropped as youngsters started voting with their feet. Rather than 'waste' the month waiting for the term to grind to a halt we introduced the idea of starting the new session's timetables on the first of June. This did result in the worn out staff having to finish the year at full throttle but it achieved a worthwhile improvement in students' attendance as they started their new courses. We were also able to set aside time for our new pupils coming up from the primaries to have a few days sampling the High

School before embarking on the real thing at the end of August.

To celebrate the end of term the Head suggested a massive all-school barbecue should take place in the playground on the last day and the staff, always up for some fun, enthusiastically pitched in. As an appeal went out for loans of barbecue equipment the cook and dinner ladies attended to the logistics, ordering vast quantities of burgers, frankfurters, and accompaniments, and arranging the setting in the playground on to which the school kitchen exited.

Several students volunteered to lend out their family barbecues and staff members were deployed to collect them on the morning of the big day. I was one on whom this duty fell, so I arranged to meet a small girl, Chloe, in the carpark just after registration, in order to fetch it from her house in Granton Road.

'It'll maybe no get in,' she muttered, looking somewhat disdainfully at my Morris Minor. 'It's quite big.'

'Oh, it'll be OK,' I assured her. 'We can leave up the boot lid if we have to.'

On reaching her house we encountered our first problem: her mother had gone to work and Chloe had no key for the main outside door which gave access to her terraced house. However we had a small stroke of luck. As we debated this problem, a neighbour exiting let us in as she left. The door led into a passageway which took us straight out to the back garden where the barbecue was kept.

Chloe's house, for which she did have a key, was on the left. She unhesitatingly made for the back garden which sloped steeply upwards and I caught my first glimpse of the makeshift barbecue, a cut-down oil barrel. One glance was enough to convince me.

'You're right, Chloe,' I gave in. 'My car's much too small.'

'What'll we do, Miss?'

'Do you have a phone we could use? We could get somebody down from the school with a minibus,' I answered.

'Yes we – oh gosh, the rabbit's escaped!'

A huge fluffy white bunny appeared, lolloping through the vegetable patch.

'We'll need to catch him,' said Chloe, scrambling nimbly after it up the incredibly steep slope.

Although we both chased after it, it was fast and frisky and only after a good fifteen minutes, during which we made havoc of the garden, did we get within grabbing distance.

'Got him!' she panted triumphantly, awkwardly clutching the fat angora to her chest and breathless and exhausted I scrambled down from a devastated cabbage patch thankful to avert an impending heart attack.

Still trembling, I held open the hutch door while she deposited it inside. After meticulously securing it we let ourselves into the house and summoned H.A. at the school.

Just as I put down the phone Chloe spoke. 'Aw Miss, Ah forgot! We're locked in! We'll need to phone ma mother to come back wi' the main door key.'

'And nobody can collect the barbecue till she comes,' I pointed out. 'We'll have to phone and tell H.A. to wait a bit!'

So we each made a call.

'We'll just have a cup o' tea while we wait,' said Chloe, making for the kitchen.

It was a weird situation. I was quite glad of the respite but very aware that time was passing. Here I was calmly drinking tea and waiting to be extricated from this student's home while everyone was feverishly scampering around back at school setting up tables and preparing to feed and amuse several hundred youngsters on the last morning of term.

'Here she comes!' announced Chloe as we finished our drinks, and sure enough her mother, still in working clothes and surprised by nothing, set us free to greet my colleague just arriving fast on her heels. With only slight difficulty we managed together to roll the barrel down the passage-way before loading it into the bus.

'Ah suppose ye'll no be wearin' these tights again,' commented Chloe with a grin as we closed the bus door, and I realised that in our frenzied rabbit chase not only had my shoes been coated in mud but my tights had been ripped to shreds.

'No,' I grinned back. 'That was quite an adventure!'

'AnnaMae's desperate to get the fire going,' announced H.A. 'She's got six hundred sausages to cook and only one other big drum!'

The panic was all hers because we knew she would do it. She was a gem. Her plump and jolly appearance belied her efficiency and along with her team of dinner ladies she was highly organised. She and I were weightwatchers, constantly struggling with excess weight, and we frequently compared notes on our progress, or more often our lack of it.

We arrived back at the school to find that, using tables, they had already fenced off an area of the back playground. Even by the morning interval when we returned, the kitchen was full of slit rolls and sliced onions, and just inside the back door a huge store of crisps, condiments and fruit juice was heaped up ready to be rolled out when the action would begin.

Self-important catering students, wearing full regalia and wide grins, were on guard, putting up bunting and helping the dinner ladies as they scurried around.

When the 12.30 bell sounded long lines of excited students assembled as usual, but outside. Chaos eventually evolved into an ingenious assembly line where students were given paper plates with burger buns which they filled with their choices: burger or sausage; onions, lettuce, and tomato; relish, mustard and ketchup.....The resulting compositions ranged from plain rolls with bare sausage to rolls filled so full that biting into them was almost impossible, but everyone seemed happy with their choice, and any leavings were soon snapped up by stray dogs.

AnnaMae seemed happy that her mission was almost accomplished, and I spied her making her way towards me carrying two boxes and laughing immoderately.

'See what I won in the Parents' Association raffle!' she exclaimed, indicating one box. She was in fits of giggles.

'What is it?' I asked, wondering how a raffle could provoke so much mirth.

'You got one too,' she spluttered, handing me the second box. 'Open it!'

Too impatient to untie the string I pulled it off and ripped open the wrapping to reveal –

'A cake!'

AnnaMae's laughter set me off too. What a coincidence that neither of us who had ever won anything before should each win a huge iced fruitcake – just what we didn't need!

However in this instance we had no need to worry about our figures; our students and colleagues descended like locusts and within minutes both cakes were history. But who cared? The warm sunshine and the prospect of the long school holidays ahead were a pleasing combination and everyone was in a happy mood.

Chapter 14

Home at Last

Not long after I retired, my doorbell rang, and I found Joe on my doorstep, not looking his best. With no sign of surprise, I invited him in. He was a boy I knew well from the school Scripture Union club I had run, but it was some time since we'd met.

'You're so grown up now!' I exclaimed. 'I haven't seen you for ages!'

'Yes', he grinned, flopping down on the sofa, 'but Ah need help!'

'Right, but would you like some tea while we talk?'

He always had been hungry and skinny, and he accepted my offer, but asked for coffee. As he eagerly attacked the coffee and some 'jammy pieces', he began to talk.

'Ken how Ah used tae stay with ma granny?' he asked.

'Yes, I do.'

'Well, when Ah left school last year Ah got a bit above maself and started gettin' cheeky.'

'Oh Joe, and she'd always been so good to you!'

'Aye. Well Ah got fed up bein' treated like a bairn. Ah couldnae get a job and she hadnae any money. She got fed up wi' me comin' in late at night, and Ah got too cheeky....'

'So what happened?'

'One night she just locked me oot and telt me she'd had enough. Ah never thought she meant it but she did.'

This was yet another sad development in a sad life – he'd almost been fated since conception. After his mother had been raped by a drunken relative, Joe had been conceived, and his mother, a lapsed Catholic, refused an abortion. Not unnaturally, his mother's husband had resented him from birth and never accepted him. By the time Joe was eighteen months old, he had had to be removed from home by social workers because of serious non-accidental injuries, before worse could befall him. That was how he'd ended up in the care of an elderly grandmother who had soldiered on, caring for him well into her eighties.

'What on earth did you do then?' I asked.

'Ah've went back tae ma mother and ma stepfaither.'

'After what he did to you as a baby! You're not safe there!'

'They're lettin' me sleep on the sofa till Ah get somewhere, but Ah ken they dinnae want me,' he replied. 'Ma brother has a nice room, but he'll no share wi' me.'

'So what are you going to do?'

'Ah went tae the Housing Department and telt them Ah was homeless, so they've given me a tenancy because Ah'm seventeen now. The Social Work gave me a bed and stuff.'

'But how will you manage for money? You've no job, and there's no dole for boys under 18.'

Jobs were very scarce: Joe had no qualifications and little to offer an employer.

'Ah've got a job in a Pakistani shop in Leith. Ah get £60 a week for 60 hours' work,' he explained. 'The money's rubbish but Ah need it tae live on.'

I realised Joe was being exploited by the shopkeeper, who was paying him pin money and providing no National Insurance protection, but what else could Joe do under the circumstances? It was commendable that he was trying to keep a roof over his head and buy the basic necessities. Now he had a house and a regular, if illegal, income but how was this inadequate seventeen-year-old boy to furnish his dilapidated flat in one of the seediest streets in Pilton?

This was the reason for his visit. He took me over to see his house, which proved to be little more than a roof over his head. Wind blew through the cracks in the windows and the dirty uncarpeted floorboards, and he had no curtains, cooker or TV set.

Fortunately, I had some useful contacts: one in particular, who worked in a lawyer's office, and was often responsible for emptying elderly clients' homes and disposing of unwanted furniture, was able to track down not only a small Belling cooker but also some curtains, rugs, a lamp, and a sagging armchair. Between us we carted these to Pilton and somehow hauled them upstairs to his first floor flat. The threadbare curtains we put up, providing him with some privacy, and Joe settled in.

He had no TV but he had prevailed on his granny

to release to him a very ancient play station, his pride and joy, and about a hundred games, which someone had dumped on him some years ago, so that would fill in his time. He thanked us for our help and said he'd keep in touch.

Sooner than I expected, only a few days later, Joe reappeared at my house, devastated.

'Ma hoose got broken into. Somebody kicked in the door when Ah was out workin'! They've taken everything.'

Sure enough, when I returned with him to his flat, it was a shambles. The insecure wooden door had yielded easily to a few kicks and all his meagre possessions had been taken, even his food. Anything left was broken and vandalised. For a few evenings he'd enjoyed entertaining friends with his computer games, even if they did help themselves and steal his coffee. Then word had got round that easy pickings were to be had here, and the vultures had descended.

It dawned on me how hopeless was Joe's quest for independent living in an area where every family kept a fierce Alsatian and no house was ever left empty, even if it meant keeping kids off school to guard it. Joe was far too vulnerable and unsupported: even the most adequate youth would have problems living alone and caring for himself in a normal environment, and poor Joe would never survive here.

'Joe,' I said, 'we'll need to find you something better than this. Let's get off to the Housing Department.'

Joe was pretty inarticulate and wanted me to be his spokesman and explain why he would have to abandon his tenancy: happily, we found the housing official quite helpful. He understood the impossibility of Joe's sustaining himself alone in the jungle of such a deprived area.

'There's this agency in Albany Street,' he said, giving me a business card. 'They're geared up to assist homeless youngsters. It might be a good idea to get down there and see if they would take Joe on.'

We went then and there and were lucky to be seen without a long wait. I had a few words with the duty worker, briefly explaining the situation, and was relieved to hear Joe was eligible for their help because he was still only seventeen, and clearly destitute. After making my goodbyes, I left Joe in their hands, and he promised to make contact soon.

True to his word, he phoned me next day.

'Miss, they've put me in a shared flat in Leith,' he reported. 'Dae ye want tae come and see it?'

I accepted his invitation and was delighted to be shown over his new home. He'd been given a furnished lockable bedsit in a four-roomed flat and was sharing a livingroom, kitchen and bathroom with three other boys. I was happy that he had privacy, security, and company when he needed it, and there was a live-in student warden who kept an eye on the boys and helped them with any problems. Joe would be trained in social skills including budgeting and cooking, and every week at a supervised flat meeting the boys could air any grievances and learn to live together.

It was a great relief to know Joe was now safe and well catered for, and I saw him several times in the next few weeks, till my usefulness dwindled and my interest in his affairs was not necessary. I was really pleased to hear he was back on friendly terms with his granny, because although she had put him out she still cared about him and he did love her. They both needed that relationship.

Almost two years passed before Joe bobbed up again, phoning to ask for help.

'Miss Smith, it's Joe,' he said. 'How are you gettin' on?'

'I'm fine. It's good to hear from you,' I said. 'How are things?'

'OK,' he replied. 'Ah'm oot the flat now I'm nineteen, and they've given me a wee place of my own, in Broughton.'

'Great! What's it like?'

'It's very nice, but there's nae cooker or bed or anything. Ah was hoping – '

'Oh yes,' I interrupted, 'of course I'll try and help!'

I drove over to see his tiny self-contained flat which was in a pleasant little square, recently redeveloped. It comprised an open-plan kitchen/living-room and a bathroom, and had been recently vacated, so it was not sparkling clean, and the previous tenant had abandoned a lot of unwanted rubbish.

After cleaning it up, we wrote a list of what Joe would need in order to move in. I was anxious to see him settled in soon because he was back, albeit briefly, staying with his mother again. Give her her due, she had provided him with some dishes and cutlery to help in the new flat, but her husband was again making it abundantly clear Joe was unwelcome in his house. We made our way to Ferry Road Drive where a large charity shop sold donated furniture at minimal prices. We were able to buy a rickety bed settee, an armchair, fridge, and a large carpet for next to nothing, and were given some basic cooking utensils, but a cooker was beyond our means. The staff of the nearby City Mission kindly lent us their van to transport these items along with a volunteer who could lay carpets, so that was a bonus!

Luckily we soon acquired a cooker from a friend

who, having just moved house, found herself with an extra one, and a sympathetic electrician installed it without charge. It's amazing what people will do when the occasion demands.

Jobs for the unskilled were still scarce, but Joe now had 'a proper job', working at the local 'co-op', and making enough to live on, so once again he set out to live alone in his new tenancy; this time, however, he had the survival skills needed and a more adult outlook, so his future was more hopeful. Joe has been out of contact now for ages, but I'm happy about that: where Joe is concerned, 'no news is good news.'

Chapter 15

A Lot to be Desired

Most of us mix almost exclusively with people of our own kind, living in closely confined social castes out of which we rarely stray. Only if our profession demands it, or through hearsay and TV, may we catch glimpses of the lives of those who want for nothing, and of those who want for everything.

Life is very much a lottery: we have no choice of our parents or our parenting, no say in the home or area where we will live, and we cannot choose to be born into riches or poverty. The lottery winners get a stable home with two loving adequate parents, and most people would regard wealth a bonus.

Those reading this could probably, in the main, be described as the luckier ones. The stories in this book may afford you some glimpses into a fairly unfamiliar world, a world peopled largely by 'unlucky ones' like Jan and Jackie, previously mentioned, who have drawn the short straw and who, through no fault of their own, live a life where deprivation and struggle are the norm.

Consider in detail some of the stark realities frequently faced by the Seans and Tracys of this world who live in substandard housing in an ill-kempt environment: their parents were failed in their youth by the education system and are consequently ill-disposed toward school; they are unskilled, poorly paid or unemployed and never have enough cash for the basics, let alone luxuries like birthday presents or days out. Many families live in constant stress with unsurmountable mental illness, domestic violence, substance abuse, or chronic illness in the home or neighbourhood, and their TV viewing continually reinforces awareness of their poverty and low social status. Of course our school did serve many poverty stricken families who had the resilience to overcome their problems, and many thoroughly supportive parents provided a valuable resource in the community. But other parents, lurching from crisis to crisis, were often unable to support their children, demonstrating the cycle of deprivation common in impoverished communities. It often seemed to us that many of our pupils' parents had probably been inadequately parented themselves and were only able to replicate in their own families all the ills to which they too had fallen prey as children.

Educationally there may well be a huge gulf between the advantaged and the disadvantaged: the latter rarely have books in the house and children are often not read to, talked to, or able to be taken out; both adults and young people may be largely marooned in their immediate neighbourhood because there is no spare money for bus fares, entry tickets, Santa's grotto, sports kit, Brownies, dance lessons and all the other leisure opportunities available. It was for this reason our headmaster and staff spent a lot of our time fund-raising by every means possible to found a unique Travel and Trust Fund for our school. This brought regular outings and residential trips within the grasp of our youngsters whose parents could barely provide them with the basic necessities, and greatly enhanced their school experience.

Research has shown that the input provided in the first five years of a child's life is extremely important – it is almost impossible to compensate youngsters whose early input may be staggeringly minimal. Children like Lizzie and Angie in Class

1L2 may start school with a vocabulary of only 100 words. How will they learn to read words never yet heard? Or relate to stories describing experiences common to the advantaged but quite foreign to them?

Children and families with multiple disadvantages come early to the attention of officialdom. Historically their general experience has been piecemeal assistance according to the needs of the moment with social work, housing, health, educational and other professionals customarily working in isolation. However, increasingly there is a recognition that a co-operative, multi-agency approach is more appropriate and the keynote is 'early intervention' rather than the 'sticking plaster' approach previously applied in crisis situations.

Research shows that tackling entrenched poverty is a complex problem which is not solvable by the mere application of money, although funds need to be available to prevent the legacy of deprivation from being passed on from one generation to the next. It is shocking that in the UK, the sixth wealthiest country in the world, 90,000 families are deemed to be living in severe poverty. Attempts to improve the situation through tax measures, grants and educational programmes have met with limited success, partly because of the complexity of the problem and partly because of the difficulty of targeting services to reach the most needy. It is the case that charities such as Barnardo's, the Child Poverty Action Group, the Joseph Rowntree Foundation, and Action for Children have done valuable research and been involved in some experimental projects, while in the last decade the Labour government has spelt out its aim to eliminate poverty by 2020.

Huge sums of money are spent in dealing with social, educational, health and public order problems relating to severe poverty: for fiscal if not compassionate reasons, governments and policy makers need to invest funds in working early and intensively with impoverished families and children, for substantial dividends could be reaped in the long term. Benefits paid out would be diminished, fewer demands would be made on the NHS, social, and justice services and many people would be making a positive contribution to society rather than living under-fulfilled lives subsisting on meagre resources provided by the state. Mike Russell, then the Scottish Education Secretary, stated in 2010 'Successive governments – local, national and UK – have recognised the importance of investing in the early years of a child's life to give them the best possible start in life we can. There is a growing body of evidence which highlights the importance of this and the positive impact which early support and intervention can have. Spending one pound on helping a child during their formative years can save the public purse up to seven pounds later on.'

Encouragingly, in 2008 the Scottish Parliament in conjunction with COSLA (the Convention of Scottish Local Authorities) launched an 'Early Years Framework' which makes a commitment to break the cycle of inequalities in health, education, and employment opportunities, through prevention and early intervention. This demonstrates a recognition of the situation, and in spite of the financial difficulties of the moment it is hoped that all the promises and purposefulness of the policy makers will bear fruit and in time transform the lot of the lowliest in our society.

APPENDIX 1

One or two facts relating to the ability and attainment of the students may help readers to understand the backdrop against which we were working.

Pupils with a reading age of less than 9.5 years on admission to the first year of high school:

1982 – 41 out of 170 admitted (24.1%)
1983 – 53 out of 167 admitted (31.7%)
1984 – 53 out of 133 admitted (39.8%)
1985 – 56 out of 115 admitted (49.6%)

In 1979 tests indicated that 66% of primary school children entering the high school were reading at a level below their chronological age. In fact, 31% of the intake was reading 21 months below the norm for their age; by 1982 this had increased to 71%, and in that year on starting high school one in six of the new entrants was reading from four to six years below his/her chronological age.

APPENDIX 2

Deprivation

Over the period 23/8/76 to 12/1/77 29 pupils were admitted to the high school, mostly because they had recently moved into the catchment area. A close look at the circumstances of these children revealed the following information.

15 of the 29 had one parent only and 3 were in care. Most of the children from single parent families were from split families. Almost all these pupils had previously attended 2 or more secondary schools before enrolling in this high school and the poor attendance of 14 of them had been a concern.

Of the 26 children living at home at least 13 of them were living on benefits because of parental unemployment.

14 of the pupils were on the free food roll.

At least 14 of the families whose children were admitted were known to the Social Work Department.

8 of those enrolled were under the supervision of a social worker.

In 7 of the families there was an alcoholism problem.

8 of the pupils were from outwith the school's catchment area, admitted at the request of social workers, parents or other schools, to give the children a new start.

16 of the children came from families where there were 3 or more children.

In addition to the above, 6 further 'problem boys' from outside the area were refused admission when requests were made by social workers and others. (These were either excludees from other schools, students just released from residential establishments, or very difficult boys on the verge of exclusion from other high schools.)

APPENDIX 3

Walter Hines Page Scholarship tour in the USA 1973

In the spring of 1973 I was fortunate enough to take up a four week travelling scholarship from the English Speaking Union in order to study 'Guidance and Counselling in the USA' with particular reference to schools in disadvantaged urban areas. During that month, in ten cities, I visited twenty-one schools and educational establishments, ranging from a senior high in downtown Manhattan with a gun-carrying cop in the hall and 5000 students (49% of whom truanted daily) to a palatial multi-million dollar high school in the second richest suburb of any US town.

Elementary and junior high schools were included in my itinerary, as were a centre for runaways in San Francisco, a lavishly endowed residential school for behaviourally disturbed students in Maryland, and one comprehensive school similar to ours, where students aged from 12 to 18 were accommodated. I also had the privilege of interviewing, amongst others, many counsellors, school principals, the director of the American Bureau of Personnel and Guidance, several people engaged in remedial and vocational programmes, several officials in the federal Education Department, and one or two county education directors.

It was something of a whirlwind tour at the end of which I would by no means set myself up as an expert on this subject. Some of what I saw and heard I have ignored as presently irrelevant or impractical in our schools, but I have tried to be constructive and positive in the following observations.

As I visited people in their homes and interviewed guidance and other personnel, I was surprised, and even amused sometimes, to find that our social and educational problems are very similar. In schools, American students face problems similar to those of their British counterparts, though often they are greater in degree (e.g. drugs, problems concomitant on a new attitude to sex, problems re personal relationships). School counsellors are facing/have faced problems in the US in becoming established as a profession similar to those currently exercising the Scots.

I intend to organise my findings into rough subject-wise divisions as follows: the role of the US counsellor and new developments in guidance; the functioning of guidance teams and their ancillaries in schools; school problems and how they are faced; the training of counsellors; and special programmes for disadvantaged students.

The counsellor's role differs from school to school, according to local circumstances and demands. Basically, as in Scotland, the counsellor exists to help students develop their full potential in school and to mature sufficiently to cope adequately and responsibly with adult life. Hitherto in secondary schools much stress has been laid on curricular guidance, and in fact this type of guidance still assumes large proportions, especially at certain periods of the school year. Educational theory, however, is swinging towards making educational practice more relevant, especially for the less academically able, and this is resulting in attempts being made to provide the student with some kind of saleable skill at the end of his school career.

For this reason counsellors are becoming more heavily involved in careers counselling, and in many schools one counsellor has vocational guidance as a major or only responsibility.

This often necessitates close liaison with local vocational schools and co-ordination with work experience programmes, set up in many schools in different shapes and forms to encourage the less able, and sometimes the less materially privileged, students to remain in school and achieve graduation with a high school diploma. I found extremely impressive careers resource centres at San Diego, with highly developed careers information and assessment programmes, and I was also interested to note, in many of the schools I visited, the existence of a close link with employers who were often prepared to give valuable help with careers education programmes.

Two interesting developments were faculty (i.e. staff) counselling and peer counselling. In some schools it appeared that the professionally trained counsellor was able to use his skills to give counselling to colleagues in regard to professional problems (e.g. student-teacher relationships). Some U.S. schools are obviously well ahead of the Scots in recognising and implementing the need for some sort of support system for the staff.

A further development of a parallel nature was the training of high school students in counselling their peers – a scheme which takes cognisance of the fact that students often turn to their fellows for advice and help when they would not approach an adult. In some localities therefore, an attempt has been made to select suitable peer counsellors and train them, rather than allow what would probably be haphazard and less effectual counselling. This situation, of course, demands close co-operation between counsellors, professional and amateur, and the issue of confidentiality requires careful handling, particularly when peer-counsellors meet problems they are unable to help with.

On this tack, it was salutary and constructive to find how many schools encouraged their students to give help to their peers in different ways: dissemination of careers information; tutoring in weak subjects; freshman orientation programmes. This would seem to generate good relationships and the sense of community responsibility so important within a school.

Within the schools, guidance teams worked closely together and regarded the school nurse, the family/school social worker, the psychologist, vocational counsellor etc. as part of the team. Many schools made it possible for students to consult counsellors of their choice rather than one allotted to them, and in the schools I visited there was evidence of a happy relationship within the student-counsellor context, informality being a keynote.

As here, relationships between counsellors and the rest of the faculty could be a problem: conversely in some schools excellent co-operation existed between counsellors and other teachers who often provided essential supportive services to the counselling team (e.g. English teachers often became heavily committed within the careers programme). In Farquhar Middle School, Montgomery County,

Maryland, the counsellors and all of the staff were involved together in a unique and progressive team-teaching situation where counselling, practical, and academic work could go hand in hand.

Another idea new to me was the concept of parent- and other aides who gave voluntary help in many different unskilled capacities, e.g. escort duty, field trip supervision, routine filing, and so on. This seemed a valuable interaction between school and community, particularly in areas of social advantage where parents were truly interested in the schools' efficient working. This was not merely confined to the guidance departments, of course, but often it was the counsellors who had generated the good rapport with the local community which promoted this. In general, from my limited knowledge of U.S. schools, it seems to me that there is a much greater parent-school contact at the one to one level than there is in Scotland and we might learn from this.

American guidance staff, trained and expected to administer many types of intelligence and aptitude tests, etc. have extensive records to keep as a result. It is interesting to find that in many schools, counsellors are given fairly substantial secretarial assistance – to allow them, as highly trained personnel workers, to concentrate on the personnel side of their work.

Problems counsellors encountered and dealt with

within the different school communities I visited are probably universal: under-achievement, truancy, illicit smoking, bullying, drugs, unacceptable behaviour, sexual promiscuity, sometimes leading to STD's or unwanted pregnancies, and so on. In all districts, whether socio-economically privileged or disadvantaged, marital disharmony, alcoholic parents, inadequate parental care or single parent families were often precipitating or aggravating factors.

The incidence of these problems naturally varies according to the local situation and in the States is sometimes affected by racial or ethnic factors (e.g. in some places where illegitimacy is no stigma there is a high rate of pregnancies amongst young unmarried students.). Clearly, in all the areas visited misuse of drugs is a more serious problem than in Scotland, and one difficult to expose and solve. One school counsellor was dealing exclusively with drug problems; in other places students were referred or referred themselves to local clinics; sometimes the school guidance team, including the nurse, dealt with the less serious cases. Girls who were pregnant were counselled, and discussed the options of abortion, marriage, adoption, or the possibility of keeping the child and remaining single. Often these students were allowed to remain in school for the full term of their pregnancy if they wished; frequently they attended special schools where prenatal care and training supplemented their normal studies; in one school a pilot project was being launched whereby girls would be afforded day nursery facilities for their children in order to allow them, as unmarried mothers, to graduate from their nearby high school.

Racial issues often overlaid and aggravated other problems: in San Francisco it was no longer possible for counsellors to administer I.Q. tests because of a court ruling that these were often verbally – and Anglo – orientated and therefore tended to discriminate against students whose first language was not English; in many schools with a wide racial mix literacy was a problem and special arrangements were being mounted to ease this situation. Counsellors, in one school at least, found it impossible to advise students against a college education – though such advice would operate in the students' best interests – because they might well have been accused of racial discrimination. Transience was also a problem with schools often having a very large annual turnover of students, up to 90% in some areas. Good communication was therefore required between counsellors, in schools in consecutive areas, in passing on information and records.

The difficulty of diagnosing mental retardation

has been sometimes been clouded by language problems impeding communication; however it is interesting to note that in some schools where there were special classes for the retarded provision was made to integrate them into the normal school programme as far as this was possible and profitable.

In the States counsellors are trained for the specific job of counselling though in many districts teaching qualifications and/or teaching experience may also be demanded. (Infrequently counsellors are part-time teachers.) In Washington State a new counsellor was provisionally appointed to a post by which time he was expected to have compiled a collection of written, visual and audio-materials to prove his fitness as a counsellor. He was afforded state certification according to the quality of proof provided and after a satisfactory interview with a 'review board' composed of one representative each from the counsellor's college, a professional association, and the local school board, respectively. Counsellors working under this system found it, initially, a constructive method of self-evaluation.

Qualifications and standards demanded of counsellors varied from state to state, and even within states, but professional bodies including the American Personnel and Guidance Association were striving to achieve greater uniformity and to establish counselling more firmly as a recognised profession, by providing a philosophy and ethics of guidance, and by laying down criteria for colleges training counsellors. These associations were also striving for more realistic working conditions for counsellors and for better public relations (e.g. the prescribed counsellor-student ratio of 1:375 was often exceeded).

Because of the demands for financial accountability currently affecting educators in various fields, it was incumbent upon many counsellors to justify monies being spent on their programmes by producing an annual multi-statistical report indicating what they were doing. Some would describe this as 'busy work' but others felt it was a useful form of self-appraisal and a means of giving others insight into their work.

There appear to be great discrepancies between educational facilities (and funding available for these) from county to county throughout the States but it was encouraging to note the trend towards federal funding of schemes which provided compensatory facilities in the education of disadvantaged children, e.g. The College Discovery Programme in New York City, and the A.B.C. (A Better Chance) in Minneapolis. In The College Discovery Programme socially disadvantaged children with a high academic potential were selected (and elected) to go into a special class in high school where they were given extra tuition and an intensive and varied programme of cultural activities which, together with special counselling help and support, enabled them to gain their high school diplomas and go on to college. (The counsellor-student ratio in this programme was 1:120 whereas the caseload of other counsellors in the school was 900 students!) The A.B.C. scheme in Minneapolis was a similar scheme on a smaller scale run by a group of philanthropic businessmen.

In Minneapolis attempts were being made to allot a greater proportion of counsellors to the downtown schools where socio-economic deprivation was common. Here the counsellor-student ratio was 1:170 as opposed to 1:360 in advantaged suburban areas. Youth Corps work programmes in which economically poor students were given paid work for several hours daily were designed partly to allow students to remain at school to graduate.

My interest was slanted towards the problems encountered in the lower socio-economic groups and amongst students handicapped by poverty, cultural deprivation, problem homes or parents, and other educationally inhibiting factors. I took the opportunity of visiting a fairly wide spectrum of schools, however, in order to see good school systems and to get a broad view of what is being accomplished in the realm of counselling. In such a short time one can only assimilate a certain amount but there is no doubt in my mind that much of what I saw and learned has been of constructive and positive value, not only in the realm of educational theory or philosophy, but practically. The whole thing was a stimulating and mind-expanding experience and I would advise anyone offered a similar opportunity to jump at the chance.

31 May 1973